The Crocodile Prize
2013 Anthology

ISBN: 0987132172
ISBN-13: 978-0-9871321-7-8

SIR VINCENT SEREI ERI (1936 - 1993)

The Crocodile, by Vincent Eri, was the first novel to be written by a Papua New Guinean, and was published in 1970 by Jacaranda Press.

Vincent was born in Moveave in the Gulf Province and later became Director of Education, PNG's first Consul General in Australia, a Member of Parliament and Governor-General.

His novel is set in Papua New Guinea before and during World War II and is a coming of age story about Hoiri, whose life poses a continuing contradiction between traditional life and the modern world.

CONTENTS

ACKNOWLEDGMENTS

We would like to thank our sponsors for 2013: Bob Cleland, the Mineral Resources Authority of PNG and Steamships Trading Company Ltd. A special acknowledgement must also go to the members of the PNG Society of Writers, Editors and Publishers who kept the Crocodile Prize alive in 2013.

Foreword

After the tumultuous political events of 2012 this year has been one of consolidation in Papua New Guinea. The government has settled down to the job of governing and to addressing major issues, such as corruption, inefficiencies in the public service and the parlous condition of state infrastructure and the delivery of health and education services.

There is a reassuring mood of stability in the country and tentative signs of improvement and better times ahead. At the same time, no one imagines that the huge task of pulling the country up by its bootstraps will be easy.

Papua New Guinea is also venturing into the international arena and is reasserting its role, along with Australia and New Zealand, as a major political and economic power in the Asian Pacific region. This is a timely development and adds a much needed Melanesian perspective to how events will evolve in the region.

Perhaps the most controversial aspect of this development has been the issue of asylum seekers and Papua New Guinea's role in processing them. This has generated widespread debate and has polarised communities in the region. To its credit Papua New Guinea has staunchly stuck to the terms of the United Nations Convention on Refugees while cleverly extracting considerable financial benefits from Australia. Together with the government's view on the control of the PNG Sustainable Development Program this approach has clearly signalled a desire by the government to be in charge of its own financial base.

One of the spinoffs of the asylum seeker deal with Australia has been the generation of publicity for Papua New Guinea and the lifting of its profile in the region.

This initially began in a highly negative form spurred on by the largely uninformed tabloid press in Australia. Slowly and surely this has turned around and many Australians who knew little about the country beyond Kokoda are now following events in a more considered way.

Domestically the events which have generated public interest revolve around the old bugbear of corruption and the unsettling escalation of violence against women, particularly highlighted by the horrendous sorcery-related witch burnings in the highlands. The draconian re-introduction of the death penalty for such crimes and other acts of violence has polarised the community. Much criticism has also been heaped on the dysfunctional and massively under-resourced Royal Papua New Guinea Constabulary. How all this evolves will be closely watched by people from within Papua New Guinea and in the region in general.

All of these issues have flavoured the efforts of the writers in Papua New Guinea, whose reach is expanding exponentially with the ever-growing facility of social media.

We hope you enjoy the short stories, poems and essays in this year's anthology.

Phil Fitzpatrick
September 2013

The Winners

During the year the *Crocodile Prize for Literature* entered its first year of administration by the newly formed Society of Writers, Editors and Publishers.

Unfortunately things did not run as smoothly as expected and the number of entries fell below those of previous years.

The reduced number of entries does not in any way diminish the quality of writing submitted to the competition however. Indeed, as the competition continues new and exciting writers continue to emerge. Some of those writers will, no doubt, take out awards in the competition in the coming years.

The society was also unable to secure sponsors for the Women's Literary Prize, the Yokomo Prize for Student Writing and the Lifetime Achievement in Literature Award. Nor could they secure a sponsor for the Writers' Workshop.

Therefore, there were only four categories where awards were available: short stories, poetry, essays and heritage writing.

As there were no heritage entries the funds for this category have been distributed to the other three.

Poetry is still by far the most popular category in the competition. The reason for this is its similarity to the traditional oral literature and songs of Papua New Guinea.

This sometimes makes the judging difficult because western-style poetry tends to be more formal and doesn't lend itself to bending the rules, unless this is done deliberately and pointedly.

The judge this year devised an innovative and objective approach based on a scoring system. It is a good model and one that will be adopted for future competitions.

The final results and winners are as follows.

Short Story

My Bougainville Prophetess by Leonard Fong Roka

Leonard Fong Roka has provided entries for the last three competitions in almost every category. Over that time he has evolved a very distinctive style of writing.

This style is characterised by the innovative use of language, not only in the selection of words, imagery and phraseology but also in the way he strings it all together. Of particular note is the way he eschews the conventional rules of grammar and invents his own way of speaking.

Leonard yields to no one in his desire to tell the story his way and sometimes the going is not for the faint-hearted.

Most writers develop a style, or use different styles, which they borrow or modify from other writer's work. Where a writer develops a distinctive and unusual style it is very rare that they use it consistently. In many cases such works are experimental. When such work evolves further it tends to become trailblazing.

Leonard's style is distinctive in that it is his own invention. However, there is nothing experimental about it. He doesn't consciously set out to write in the manner in which he does but his writing is largely instinctive and comes from somewhere deeper. One suspects that, in part at least, it has had its genesis in the Bougainville conflict, about which he so elegantly writes. Whatever the source, it has evolved into something that other writers can only envy. It might also be added that it takes courage to do your own thing, especially in literature.

In this sense it is difficult to identify his influences, or, in fact, if there are any. At the moment his writing defies description, except perhaps for its raw and visceral aspects. *My Bougainville Prophetess* is an example of his writing that illustrates a stage in an evolution that promises great things as it matures further.

His short stories are gritty and uncompromising, providing insights for the reader even as he works to exorcise some of his own demons through his writing.

The characterisations are strong, the narrative is fresh, the twists and turns are gripping.

Leonard's writing is also refreshing because it promises much for the literature of not only Bougainville but also for Papua New Guinea and the greater Melanesian realm. In his work he is setting an example for other Melanesian writers to follow. In time this may even develop into a distinctive regional style. It's greater value, however, is to demonstrate the possibilities for others who might follow in his footsteps.

It is for these reasons that he has been selected as the best short story writer for 2013.

His winning entry appears on page 22.

Poetry

I am woman by Lapieh Landu

The judge in the poetry category identified four very strong contenders for the prize. Lapieh's poem just pipped the others at the winning post.

Those others were *As A Writer* by Diddie Kinamun, *A Faceless Silhouette* by Pamela Toliman and *Melanesian Woman* by Jessica Dobb. We hope to hear more from these three poets in 2014.

Lapieh has been a strong and consistent poet since the inauguration of the competition. She has a keen sense of herself and her people with a parallel sharp intellect to express her thoughts and emotions. Despite it being a close competition she is a worthy winner.

Her poem is made up of excellent couplets containing a

question that is answered at the end. The short, almost terse responses are confident and proud. The diction in the poem is very strong and each couplet is a gem of description. All in all, her poem is presented in a simple format which is very effective and very well expressed.

Of the other three poems the judge offered the following comments which are worth recording.

Diddie Kinamun's poem contains startlingly vivid images with well-developed verses. There are major turns in the poem, from ancient carver to modern writer to the current problems faced by the new generation of 'cultural scribes'. This poet deserves our attention.

Pamela Toliman's poem struck the judge as 'two words over the mark of perfection'. The terse and direct prose evokes strong emotions of the time in history that it is set and the description is crisp and precise. Such writing will preserve the memory of people during those times.

Jessica Dobb's poem is a light-hearted yet proud poem celebrating Melanesian women, especially at this difficult time in Papua New Guinea. The image it conjures is true and it exhibits excellent use of rhyme with a very neat start and strong finish.

Lapieh's winning poem appears on page 66. The others are on pages 61, 71 and 49 respectively.

Essay

If Dekla Says Papua New Guinea is Eden, Then It Is! By Francis Nii

This essay is a direct but very unique response to the negative publicity that Papua New Guinea received in the Australian media following the announcement of the deal to process asylum seekers on Manus Island.

Rather than a predictable diatribe about the insensitivity of the Australian media the essay takes a much gentler course and uses humour and homespun wisdom to demonstrate that life for many Papua New Guineans, particularly in rural areas, is, in fact, very good. It also pokes fun at those Papua New Guineans who slavishly follow westernised ways without realising what their own traditional cultures and lifestyles have got to offer.

The end result is an anecdote and fable of considerable power, both in its social and political contexts. Part of this power is in its purposeful but cleverly disguised objective of making its readers think about the issues. In this sense it follows in the footsteps of the great essay writers and is a worthy winner.

His winning entry appears on page 126.

SHORT STORIES

Bagolu Kainali - The Sound of Waves
Alfred Eliesa Faiteli

The silvery October moon gradually emerged from the sinking horizon mellowing its silvery rays on the placid waters of the Pacific Ocean. Tonight was somewhat different, splendid yet unnerving unlike the previous nights. The water was still, the sky luminous and the air eccentrically filled with the sharp scent of wet seaweed, dried coral, the fresh stringent aroma of *siyales* and the monotonous sound of crashing waves which made this night quite unique; one never to forget easily.

Topeula stood outside his coconut frond thatched hut speechless, gazing into the open sky in deep thought. One could tell that his thoughts were not confined to the vicinity of his island home but those that extended far beyond the horizon. In front of where Topeula was standing, were several fallen coconut trunks, a pandanus and a *keyalu* tree submerged in the sea, uprooted by the rising seas. In display and despair, their roots exposed the calamities of the devastating impact of climate change on small fragile island community. Tonali was no exception.

Tonali is home to a small but vibrant Melanesian population, once viewed as a beautiful island paradise located in the middle of the western Pacific whose people depend on the sea for their livelihood and a matrilineal solidarity that formed the basis of their existence. Without the sea, Tonali and Tonalians would never exist. Amidst the dire straits of its current plight, the islanders have always hoped for a brighter future. A future challenged by climate change, time and development.

Tonali is caught in this dilemma. Its flora and fauna, culture and people are placed in a most vulnerable situation, more so now, than ever before. Evidence of such destruction is obvious. Ten years ago, the old village site was located about seven metres from the shoreline, but is now covered by water where only a few *paoli* posts stand idle, rotting with the passing of time. All the other landmarks of the past have been erased by changes portending a future that is gloomy and volatile.

Were these some of the many thoughts that were bombarding Topeula's mind tonight?

From a distance, the faint voices of women could be heard as they moved quietly and urgently in the dim light of hurricane lamps. Outside, one could see shadows of the night and moon as they blended into imaginative creations of ancestral spirits dancing to the rhythm of the sea breeze and the slow rustling of dried *gawam* leaves.

It was beginning to get cold.

Topeula stretched his arms and then ambled further along the beach away from his hamlet, still keeping his eyes towards the open sky. He found a quiet spot on the sandy beach and sat down facing the ocean. One could tell that the multitude of questions that were flooding his mind was becoming unbearable and he waited impatiently, anticipating an answer to put him at ease. This however seemed a long time-coming and he stared towards the moonlit sky as if expecting the answers to fall from the twinkling stars.

The moon climbed higher into the sky in its full splendour. Topeula's eyes began to be filled with tears. One by one, these tears trickled slowly down his cheeks. Dark grey clouds began to cover the moon followed by the poignant kwaaaking of a crow, which made Topeula jump to his feet. There was then silence. Nothing moved. Only the continuous sound of the waves as they gently unfolded on the shore. Something was not quite right.

Suddenly, *iiiieeee...iiiieeee...* the sound of crying was heard coming from Topeula's hut. Listen! The cry of a newborn child. Immediately, Topeula turned and dashed towards the house. He darted his way towards the door and peered into the room only to be led away by Meleka. *"No...no...,"* he yelled, breaking the stillness of the moonlit night. *"No... I want to see Waikena,"* he protested. *"Waikena...my Waikena,"* he cried as he was led to the *patapata*. *Tawae kaiwena ku logabaegau? O...Waikena!"* he broke down and wept bitterly and unstoppably, comforted by Meleka and other relatives who by now had come out of their houses to confront the anguishing situation.

As the cry of the newborn child echoed through the night, so did the mourning chants of Topeula and his close relatives. In front of them, on a pandanus-woven mat laid the outcome of the complicated delivery – Waikena. She was dead. Close to her, her baby, moving his arms vigorously to grasp and feel the warmth and love of his mother and suckle the milk from her breast; truly a heartbreaking sight. Within moments, Meleka, Waikena's elder sister entered the hut, crying as she embraced Waikena and took the child into her arms, chanting her mourning song followed by the other womenfolk.

As the message of death passed through the island, doors began to open; lights began to flicker and people began to move quietly, gathering at Topeula's big house. They all came in numbers as news spread across the village to share this experience; ironically, one that encompassed both life and death; death - in the passing of the moonlight season and life - expressed in the sound of waves.

This happened on the 11th day in the month of October, 1990.

I grew up beside the sea. For me, the sea has become who and what I am. Being able to read the flow of tides and identify the different sea currents and their directions by day and night now form an integral part of my knowledge as an islander. I remember those childhood days, together with my cousins, Sineka and Timota, when we would set sail in our small dug-out canoes with pandanus sails during the *siwaloi* season enjoying the life of being island children.

I also recall the day I was initiated. Ushered by my uncles to the *numetau* dressed in traditional *sivi*, the old men chanted sacred words and blew from their mouths *sala-seala* spittle to ward off bad spirits. After I entered the *numetau*, they thumped their *sidais* and farewelled my adolescence in rhythmic dancing and singing. This traditional ritual signified the transition from adolescence to adulthood.

Sad to say, the social fabric of this once vivacious island society has gradually crumbled. Tonali has lost its purpose, not only in its culture but also in its natural beauty and its drive to make this place hospitable, liveable and sustainable. Many Tonalians have moved to bigger and faraway places in search of better lives. Why they have never returned? I do not know.

As I sat in my dormitory reminiscing on this particular day, a peculiar feeling overwhelmed me. It was not until later that morning I found out why. Tonali had been hit by a devastating tsunami the previous night. All that was left were a few houses and families. One hundred and forty people were reported dead and fifty missing; among them, papa Topeula and mama Meleka. My heart sank as I remembered the final words of Topeula: *"Will you ever come back to Tonali again?"*

It was on this unforgettable day, 15th of October 2010, outside Mr. Sonoga's office, that I made my final decision.

As I strolled on the sandy shores of Tonali on this glorious night a week after leaving school, I rediscovered the fate of this land expressed by its emptiness. No sense of life could be felt in this once lively island environment. I remember as children running on this beach, barefoot; laughing and giggling as we chased our serene shadows under moonlit skies. I looked around, no one was there; truly a state of psychological turmoil, utterly depressing and disturbing.

These memories have now become dim recollections in

my mind. What I vividly remember though are family faces and familiar spaces of my life. Many wonderful people I knew and loved have passed on from *meagai* to a peaceful resting place. Only their footprints remain in the shifting white sand on which I stand. Although they have gone, I feel the presence of their spirits around me – warm and cold.

As I look into the sky, I capture in full view the October moon rising above the horizon in its most majestic form like I have never seen before in my entire life. Suddenly, within me a rekindling spirit of optimism began to emerge. I now make my final decision: to be laid to rest in my *meagai* land, next to w*aikena* – my mother. This shall be my final resting place.

I wade into the sea, breathe a sigh of relief and smile long into the night with teary eyes as a sense of new hope and assurance grips my heart and soul.

Now I knew who I was - who I am – in this life and in death.

Siyales – frangipani.
Keyalu – casuarina.
Paoli – mangrove.
Gawam – okari.
Patapata – wooden platform for sitting on.
Tawae kaiwena ku logabaegau? – Why did you leave me?
Siwaloi – calm
Numetau – traditional men's house.
Sivi – costume.
Sala-seala – betel nut and ginger.
Sidais – wooden drum.
Meagai – motherland.
Waikena – moonlight.

The Ragged Face at the Traffic Light
Diddie Kinamun Jackson

It was a bright Saturday afternoon and we were just coming back from a Graduation Ceremony. We were all merry from the family outing, Dad was at the wheel, Mum was in her usual place beside him and I sat in the back seat with my aunt.

My brothers were at home; left behind because Mum and Dad said they were a headache, "uncontrollable males", typical of those boys.

We went as we were without the rest of the clan. In a way it was good because we had peace of mind without a noisy bunch, a great relief for me.

The ceremony was great. As would any parent who had a child graduating from University, they were happy for their child. We headed for home at 7 pm. On the way Mum was nagging Dad about this and that and everything else that came to her mind, you know, wanting to know everything.

In this kind of situation I just hate listening to their crap, so I just pushed the earpieces blasting music deep into my ear canals.

Dad wanted to shut Mum up so he drove like hell, which was very scary but in a way good at this point in time because Mum was frightened of speeding cars, or anything that has wheels and moves fast, so she shut her mouth so Dad would drive at a normal pace. I was glad she did but I know she is always right in what she says, God bless her soul.

Suddenly we came to an abrupt halt as Dad hit hard on the brakes at the traffic lights. Dad was a bit drunk and nearly ran into the red light sign. He was cursing Mum. It was fun to watch them argue in the friendly way that they did.

The green light came on and as we were about to go Dad said sharply, "Give me some coins! Give me some coins!"

I pulled the earpieces out of my ears and popped my head up trying to hear and see what the commotion in the car was about. Then I saw a small huddled little figure with a dirty shirt placed in front of him sitting patiently waiting for any kind hearted person to throw him some loose coins. My heart melted as we searched frantically to find some coins to give him while the other cars were hooting their horns at us. Sadly Dad drove away.

Dad felt bad I knew and Mum was quiet as we drove away. There were all sorts of thoughts running through my head, "What if that was one of my brothers?" I closed my eyes tightly trying to block the image of the ragged figure from my mind's eye. Silent tears swelled. The thought of not giving him anything made me feel even more guilty. He looked to be only ten or twelve years old, trying to fend for himself.

His image disturbed me all night and I knew in my heart that he needed help. Oh how I thank God that I was blessed in having a loving family and food on the table. That ragged dirty face taught me a valuable lesson; whatever little I had it was plenty enough because someone more needful was out there somewhere.................

Bantoka Place
Leonard Fong Roka

"So…so, here you are come back," old Dentana is happily welcoming his grandson. "So quick you made it Maate. I last saw you at the market; or maybe at the junction of Kereitu Street. I am not sure with my memory because of my age. Was it where your uncle lives a few streets up at Section 15, Asita Street, just in the vicinity of your school, Tupukas Primary."

Maate sits in the room admiring the family photographs, framed and neatly hanging, scattered across the wall. So many there are; Grandpa smiling in his teens; Grandpa and Grandma in Honiara; Grandpa and Maate at the abandoned Panguna mine in the 1980s and on and on the list goes.

Standing against the wall opposite the window is the festooned Madonna. "This is a real sanctum," Maate is whispering to himself. "Why am I here Grandpa?"

Nobody knows that though. Grandpa has every photograph he owns in the room that Maate is occupying while he is attending school. Grandpa has also chosen the school for him to attend - the very school that his aunties attended so many years ago.

The reasons are Grandpa's alone but deep down Maate knows why his grandfather favours him so much. It is because his looks are those of his grandma. This is why Grandpa takes him for his blue-eyed boy. He loves him the most and often prays for him with his rosary for his success in life.

Without a door is Maate's room, only Grandpa's has one. Passing from the entrance, he goes to the end of the wall that separates his room from the dual purpose lounge and dining room adjoining the tiny kitchen. He had been exploring to see what the old man is doing; stirring up chinking sounds and talking to himself.

"Kaaka, what you doing?" he asks, after a brief moment of hesitation.

"Preparing a little chowder just for you, kaaka," the feeble voice in the kitchen is calling back. "Would you mind running up to Section 16 Tonguru Street - there's a canteen there - and get a packet of rice? The money is there on the table behind you." Dentana is pointing at a table that occupies almost 30 percent of the lounge-dining room.

Maate carefully makes his way through the dirty puddle-infested Bantoka Street. He knows that many years ago this street was wide enough for two cars to run side by side. Today, creeping thorny grass, called *dongasi* in the Kieta language, and other creepers and plants have squeezed it to a mere one and half metres wide.

"Hi, Maate, you are at school here now?" disabled Tonama, is asking while busying his lips with his mouth organ and somehow talking at the same time.

With just a nod of his head, Maate ambles on.

The giant Pikus tree captures his attention, so he slows down as a car speeds up the Rumba Road. Its tyres screech loudly as it passes Doraka Street ahead.

"Stop admiring that damn tree," Jackie says, approaching him.

She is a teenager and, unlike him, a Basikanung of the Kurabaang clan. One of the clans his traditions permits him to marry into. Furthermore, her accent suggests that she is from the Panguna area. She is one of the Ioroan love singers of the rugged mountains.

"Just admiring the view," Maate is frankly saying.

"That's a waste of time; acting like a tourist. Soon you will be admiring the view of me," Jackie says with a mocking laugh and saunters on slowly. Then she adds: "Right in my room."

"Thank you. And, when?"

"When time permits, my boy," Jackie says. They venture on their separate ways in suspense.

A swollen shopping bag dangling in hand, Maate is standing outside the screen door rubbing dirt from the soles of his shoes on the worn flood mat. From the kitchen, and permeating through the air, is the delicious smell of food that is making him hungry. So he enters with high hopes of tasting Grandpa's stew.

"Oh Maate, the stew is being cooked," Grandpa says as he licks a spoon like a child. "Now, it's your turn to boil the rice."

The sun is setting over the western ridges as the afternoon breezes set in with steaming calmness and the pair is comfortably sitting around the dinner table, spoons chinking and tingling on the fragile glass bowls.

The meal is perfect to the oldie, who considers himself, the best cook around Kieta. "Maate, is this stew made by an old bone okay?" he asks joyfully.

"Very nice," Maate is saying, decanting the final remains of his bowl into his wide mouth. He is a glutton.

"Tha...n...k you," the oldie, says with a sort of grogginess to Maate's surprise.

"Kaaka, what is it?" says the grandson, fearfully.

"Not...hing," the old man twitches, sweeping his plate to the floor. Then, the wriggling body lands with a bang next to it. For minutes, he struggles there as the grandson stands like a guard affixed by fright. His mouth is wide open and saliva is trickling down his fat lips.

Recollecting his senses: "Finis?" Maate is staring at the grizzled head; then he bends to check if there is still a pulse. Alive, he discovers. His heart is beating loudly.

Maate wets him with a moist tea-towel and he comes to his senses. He assists him to a chair.

"You know, my child," the sick fella sobs in self-pity, "I've completed me gradation in life; and this life is at the brim ready to go. That's why I suffer a lot with ailments like trances and many others." He pauses in thought. Then adds, "But this house is what I don't want to lose …." Something distracts him. He is thinking?

"Don't want to lose, why?" the youngster is prompting to squeeze out the reasons.

"This old house, Maate, is where my life was moulded. From here I got your grandma, whose death denied her the joy of growing old together with me. Your mother and uncles and aunts were born here. Here is where, our spirits belong." His eyes water but he continues. "Because of my intense love for this domicile - after the Bougainville crisis - I reclaimed it for you; for in you, your grandma dwells, so there is light at the end of the tunnel in you. He looks around the room, then adds in finality, "In case, if you need to know, this house is on Section 14. The house, on the maps of Arawa, is numbered 143 and it is located on Bantoka Street. If you sell it, you will disadvantage yourself."

Maate is lost for words seeing this very intimate bond between the old man and the house. He is thinking how his grandpa left home and migrated into town after the war. "So, Grandpa is only going back home in his coffin," he is telling himself. Back at home, in Paraiano, his kinsmen are calling him and are waiting for him and his coffin.

Night time cicadas and other insects are shrilling outside. Added to the disturbances is the howling of dogs in their mating and the wind was blowing the branches of the mighty Pikus tree to and fro sending ripe seeds onto the rooftops with unpleasant thudding sounds. Thud upon thud until Maate begins his session of profound snoring in resistance.

A remarkable fortnight is just whistling by. A memorable fourteen days; one of them - a pleasant Tuesday - witnessed Maate losing his dogged virginity to the *kurabanang*, Jackie, of house number 171 in Doraka Street. So swiftly the days are fading, just like the shooting stars in the night sky.

Since his arrival in town, Maate knows that his grandpa's life is hanging on a thread - ready to go. The fact that he lives in this beloved little red house is jam-packed with the disturbing trepidation of finding himself sleeping under a single roof with a dead man. This goads him into regularly overnighting across the road in Asita Place. In the mornings he lies to the old fella, saying that he took refuge from molesting drunks and other reasons that are too many and are absorbed by the old man grain by grain.

But on this fateful night, muffled up in a thick blanket, is Maate, struggling against the cold in this strange morose darkness. He is feeling spirits from distant places hovering around his grandpapa in an angelic dance. Fuggy is the air. Sweat begins to trickle down his body so he unwraps and gropes his way outside to be welcomed by two fireflies orbiting merrily around the veranda post. He knows that fireflies are the agents of death.

"Kaaka, is it you and Tete?" he asks the fireflies as he passes to a seat on the moist lawn.

In the open, he feels safe from the spirits' daring plucks. But his belief in fireflies as the actual physical form of death is confusing him. He is now watching their airborne strutting, like a boy transfixed by a nymphet, as they are disappearing behind the house. And to his surprise, they are dancing around him again; bumping into his side restlessly. Other straying mates are also teaming up for this ritualistic masquerade. Then, seemingly bored they are now withdrawing, leaving behind a lone fly that orbits around Maate twice and then departs as the first cock crow in the neighbourhood begins before dawn.

The sun is high as the morning breeze peacefully blows sleep out of the abodes of Arawa. The sky is cerulean, like the sea and Maate is lying embraced in sleep beside the flower bed. A neighbour sees him and wakes him up.

"Hey, Maate why are you asleep here?" he asks.

"I just wanted to," he lies as he rubs off dirt from his side and dashes into the house to wake the old fella.

He goes to his grandpa's door to confirm his nightmare. His left palm firmly grips the door knob, turns it to set the door ajar and hesitantly peeps in. He carefully looks at the resting figure. The old man's chest is not moving up and down with the intake of fresh air and the unleashing of waste air out. "Kaaka, are you still sleeping?" he asks, but no answer comes. Instead, an ant creeps out of the old man's nostril; he is dead. Peacefully dead in the house that he loved the most.

Maate is rushing out of the room. "Kaaka, why did you do this to me?" he is wailing. "Why did you desert me?" He is rolling and singing a mourning song on the gravel and dirt of the lawn and sympathetic neighbours are rushing in to comfort him.

Early the next morning, Maate sits in the open back of a Land Cruiser in a convoy of cars bringing home his grandpa's casket. A red Hilux is carrying the casket in front as the others follow behind. Slowly, they climb up Ako Hill on the eastern-most fringe of Arawa in suffocating diesel fumes.

"Kaaka, you loved the little red house numbered 143 on Bantoka Street," Maate is saying to himself. "I will, however, love the little green house numbered 171, where Jackie dwells in Doraka Street. That's where my spirit is locked."

The convoy is hidden by the bend at Karukate; Arawa is gone from Maate's sight and slowly, they descend down Keuru brae and onto the coconut palm-covered Kereinari plains

Kaaka – grandfather/grandson in Nasioi language.
Tete – grandmother.

Farewell My Bougainville Prophetess
Leonard Fong Roka

The stench of body odour and sweat poisoned Dabuna's psyche as she jostled her way through the flesh of high spirited travellers in the Buka airport departure lounge. On her tail was her proud mama, Itonani, who braved her way through the curious eyes of the black men hanging onto the windows silently saying goodbye to their fellow countrymen and countrywomen.

Laborious was the posture of the queue for the check-in counter but the joy for a daughter going to the foreign land of *erereng* to be educated belongs not in the pocket. It was something to be expressed by being beside her daughter, steadfast till she was airborne.

Dabanu, the great woman of Kongara, secured her boarding pass with a dancing heart, for going away from her Bougainville in an air plane to study and become a teacher was a milestone. She hugged her grey haired mama and together they took an edge of a bench and sat.

"Dabanu, my daughter," she consoled her baby as they sat waiting for the big bird to land, "you are the light of those backward and barbaric mountains of Kongara. The Kieta people blame us for all the trouble that happens in Arawa; but it is us that saved their land from the cruel erereng that dug a big hole in the heart of our island with their big company, that thieving Bougainville Copper Limited".

"Kietas are like that, mama," Dabanu cried, as she got herself hunched ready in a corner near the boarding gate, "They think we are the scent of trouble in the land. But it was us who died to fight those ever thieving erereng that were colonizing our land and minds."

Out of no-where the plane roared as it landed upon the Bougainville soil. It taxied to a stunning halt to their north

22

and, with a quavering roar again it entered the clear space before them. The pair watched in wonder as the airport men maneuvered to and fro, doing their jobs.

It was white and so imposing. Dabanu had a thorough look at it as people began to enter the terminal as swift as eagles. On it were the symbols - a Bird of Paradise and the words, 'Air Niugini' - of the distant country and people that had ruled their land since that fateful year, 1975.

"Mama, *si damaiko simenang*," her mama hugged her as tears rolled down her aging cheeks. "*Tampa sikuru darabaing*, Bougainville, the land your brothers and sisters died for needs you".

"Don't worry mama," Dabanu consoled, fighting off tears.

"My daughter," Itonani sobbed, "you are the future of your clan; you are the mother of the land of Tairima and you are the blood of Bougainville's future for which our people from Buka to Buin have died and suffered for under the terror of the cruel *erereng* since the days of the Germans.

"Be careful and never wander away from your school for the land of the *erereng* is a land of rapists, rascals, murderers and false gods - men of the street that preach till night. Yes, daughter you know it as the newspapers tell us who these people are. They did the same in our land so we had to fight and chase them away and now we enjoy our freedom on our island".

The mother and the daughter were still clinging to each other in the deep sorrow of losing each other. The other travellers began jostling through the exit for the plane that was waiting outside in the shimmering heat of the day.

"My daughter," the saddened mother, sobbed, "please remember those word of your uncle Birengka as he farewelled you at Kakusira. He said, 'As populations increase, our land is not expanding and this means land has a store of conflicts for you, Dabanu. So you have to marry a man who knows your myths and family history. This is a man from a clan our family has marital relations with since the dream times. My niece, this is your power to laugh off liars."

Itonani let go of her daughter and helped her with her handbag and tidied her tangled shirt at the collar.

"Remember your father," the sorrow shaken mother added as an afterthought, "he died for the good of our land and your future as a Bougainvillean on Bougainville and not a nobody. Love not an alien that does not know your myths and will not stand to support you when conflicts arise because he is stranger without roots in Bougainville or Choiseul where your progenitors come from."

Dabanu, with tears running freely down her cheeks, marched for the exit broken hearted. She was now leaving her beloved mother in tears, a sin she hated. The mother who had brought her up without a father because he had been killed by the *erereng* army as he fought for their rights to be Bougainvilleans.

Her mother was her life. Her mother was all the reason for her existence through the war that the erereng had fought so they could steal Bougainville's wealth and resources.

"Be educated my love, and come back and help Bougainville to be free." The last words of her beloved mother echoed in her head as she entered the plane.

Directed to a seat, she sat in tears looking out of the window. The plane rattled towards the runway and after a few seconds she was high in the sky like an eagle; but this was an eagle, she seemed to be comfortable with.

As the northern tip of Bougainville faded from sight, she was mesmerized by the beauty of Buka Island as it drifted below on the vast blue sea of Solomon. Her land was truly a paradise of black people.

Her flight was scheduled for a stop-over in Rabaul so she kept her eyes to the sea below.

Buka was gone from her sight, now there was no island

in the blue sea below. She wondered why her Bougainville was called 'one country' with the Papua New Guineans when there was no proof of closeness between them.

She remembered her flight from Taro airport to Honiara some years back. It was so beautiful how her Bougainville was connected to Choiseul, Santa Isabel and Guadalcanal. But now she was lost. The Papua New Guineans had indoctrinated Bougainvilleans with all the lies they had adopted and created for their own country.

The plane merged into some turbulence that surprised her. Below she could not see any further because of the thick clouds. So she mumbled a prayer to God for her safety on the plane and in the land of the strangers ahead.

Warm tears rolled down her cheeks as she envisaged her mother sitting and crying at the Buka runway.

"Dear God," she prayed in tears. "Protect and guide me for I am the mother of Bougainville; a Bougainville woman who is still in pain and in need of freedom. Let me be the light of the future for my people who perished in the war against exploitation and those who are still forced to dance to this exploitation and indoctrination. Amen."

Erereng — 'redskin' in the Nasioi language.
Si damaiko simenang — Oh, you are leaving me, my love.
Tampa sikuru darabaing — commit yourself to your studies.

I am going back to my roots
Leonard Fong Roka

Bali Bris, Kimbe. It is here, by the soothing sounds and smell of the sleepy Bismarck Sea, I am beseeching my soul to tell me 'where is my Bougainville?' Where am I heading to after all the years in the Solomon Sea?

But here I am, I have taken a step with a stinging pain in my heart to carry on across this unpredictable sea in the cover of the falling night.

I am going to Bali, West New Britain, the birthplace of my father. I am going to see my broken hearted grandmother whom has being wishing and weeping to see me before she follows her dear son to the tomb. But I am going empty handed and not with the remains of my father whom I have killed on Bougainville.

I am going, after years of weeping silently to see and set my feet on that mystery in the Bismarck Sea. I am going with a broken heart.

My *toto* [aunt] keeps telling me the tales of this mystery sea and our island, Bali, somewhere in the midst of this expanse of sea before my eyes. She talks about the beauty of the night from this dancing trawler before us; the shoal of flying fish and drifting logs on the way to the Witu islands makes a voyage memorable. She is singing.

'Ever you cross the sea, *toto*?' *toto* enquires.

With my eyes on the silhouetted Kimbe Island, I can only nod, 'Never, never and never' accompanied by a distant chuckle.

'Poor you, *toto*,' *toto* laughs.

The Rastafarian wheel-man of our trawler, MV *Kathleen*, passes before us with a mouthful of areca-nut and gives a distant thumps-up to his crew man who just shines so bright in smile of the sea. They are the sea because they love the sea that I fear because Panguna in Bougainville has no sea for me to love.

Then comes a casket, they said was a relative of mine who had died in Moresby. He was a chief of a place they said was Penata on Bali Island where I belong, too. He was so beautified with flowers and clean clothing wrapped him to sleep for the night long journey.

My *toto* ushers me forward for the tiny ship. I am lost. I think about giant of waves of the sea people talk about. I fear that a sea rage upon us would be worst when we have a casket onboard. But I had no hope; I have to go across this sea of mystery that my papa's people love so much.

My *toto* shakes my hands and wishes me a safe trip home to Bali.

I make my way to the back and secure a position on a petrol drum. I love this spot so much just to see and admire the foamy water that is stirred by the drive propellers beneath the hull.

From here I take on a good view of the few people I am with for this voyage. There are three mothers with tear stain eyes; there is a cackle of colleens who keep smoking and chewing betel nut and there is a trio of ship staff men who march about like hovering house flies.

The little Kathleen throttles and quakes. Smell of diesel fumes blankets us as one of the people on the wharf, whom I can only see his feet above us, removes the mooring line and hands it over to the crew who greedily hides it where it belongs.

The ship is going down the river cutting through drifting debris, tin cans that humans litter in the Kimbe town. I watch the town fading. The huge oil palm tanks that stand too proud in the skyline of the Kimbe town grow smaller every second as I feel like crying for leaving land for the mercy of this great river. But I am okay, for I have had left Bougainville to set my feet on that island in the midst of the Bismarck Sea.

A boy comes to me. 'Brother, don't you worry. The villagers will cry over you for you are bringing your late father back to his island of birth'. He makes me shed a tear.

I lower my head and fight back tears. My eyes fixed on the palm infested Talasia coast to the west which our Kathleen is navigating parallel to for the Bulu Point up north. I wondered if a god was there on Mount Hela to redeem me from this pain. I look upon Mount Bere, but it is snoring. I skim up the Mount Habuna for a god of peace, but there are none here since Bougainville is a stranger to them.

A shoal of flying fish disturbs me. I look into the water as they submerged into eternity of the sea. Then I look back at Kimbe but she is now a dot for we have made distance pass the Garua Plantation at Talasia Station. I am making it fast into the unknown mystery of the sea.

As the ship decreases the distance to Bali every hour, I am weeping more and more, deep in my heart. But I am going; going with a broken heart and empty hands for my withering New Guinean grandmother.

The Mount Vakori, the tallest of the Talasia Peninsula, pities not a lost Bougainvillean tourist. It keeps on torturing me: 'Where is my kin? Where is my blood? Where is my son, you killer Bougainvillean?' I had no strength for a fight so I let tears run freely down my cheeks and hide in my jacket to sneeze.

Kathleen conquers the Talasia Peninsula at Bulu and rain falls with lightening. Night settles in and cold penetrates the marrow of my bones. I look out to sea, but there is no life except the flicker of lightening above us.

The boy whom my Kimbe toto has ordered to take care of me is always around for me giving me strength and a peace of mind with his stories and areca nut. We are a family of mourners around the coffin which we all were positioned around with.

A single light are put on to illuminate and a Rastafarian mother cuddling her sleeping child looks me hard. She calls the boy who had being orbiting around me for so long and asks, 'Who is this stranger?'

After their short chat the world awakes. 'People; people, we have onboard two chiefs of Penata, 'she weeps in a strange language of my father's people. Pointing at my position she says: 'There is Mataio, our living chief who has come across the sea from Bougainville and here is our death chief of Penata'.

She slams the coffin and weeps hysterically and added, 'Toto; my toto, why have you come when I am moaning?'

I shed tears and gave her my back. My minder also shed tears as sorrow creeps into our midst. The rain eases and sea is pacified by our broken hearts. And our vessel churns on proudly in the darkness our eyes could not penetrate.

But our trawler gallops on with confidence against my doubts of arriving home in harmony with the mystery sea.

By dawn my eyes become heavier with the stress of the long sleepless journey as I sat on a drum. But I fought away the bothering sleep to watch the sea and listen to the hisses of torturing upon a lost Bougainvillean tourist.

As the sun began to chase away the dark, islands appear and I am told that they are the Witu group. Our *Kathleen* braves its way far south from them as it headed straight for Bali somewhere in this midst of a sea expanse beyond my expectations.

People who had occupied the front of the wheel house saw it first and my guardian angel came close and lectures me. 'Brother, those are the Kumburi sister mountains of your land'. But I saw no mountains and wondered. But as the vessel steamed closer, it was true; really they were mountains so steep.

My minder kept talking. 'On the other side of these mountains are your homes Makiri, Manopo, Penata, Nigilani and the land of Vamangama. Our only running river is Boroko that is sourced on the foot of the Kumburi Mountains. From Manopo, you will come and we can play at the Nughutu islet and cove or we can paddle to our fishing and hunting island of Ragha to hunt for wild pigs and birds. It's fun there'.

'Yes, toto,' the Rastafarian toto hugs me and weeps, 'this is your island. This is where I cared for you many years ago when you were a child with your late father and mother'.

I cannot control the emotions in my heart and warm tears profusely began running down my cheeks. I was crying for coming empty handed for my withering grandmother and my home of Bali Island.

Brothers Until the End
Ephraim Toirima

Two boys of the same age lived in the same neighbourhood. They grew up together playing every day, sleeping over at each other's house and having fun as kids do. They were the best of friends and no matter how they played and fought over toys and games, like kids do they still ended up laughing and smiling at the end.

On their first day of school, although their parents had enrolled them together, they were put into different classes. The two would sneak into each other's classroom when the teacher was not around and play and have fun causing a lot of nuisance. The teachers in the school eventually gave up and allowed them to be in the one class.

The boys were the best of friends, they would go to school together in the mornings, help each other out during lunchtime with food; splitting ice blocks in half so that each had a share. When trouble found them, they stood back to back in fights with the other boys and triumphed over them because two was always better than one.

Together they graduated from Primary School and were selected for the same High School. The boys faced lots of challenges because High School was a new environment; binge-drinking, drug addiction, sexual relationships and peer pressure nearly crumpled their friendship. They each had girlfriends at school but whenever the other needed anything, the girls became a memory for their brotherhood was much stronger.

Both grew up and became men. After the hardships of High School they prospered and went to the National High School. They together met much greater problems, such as the loss of one of the boy's mother through cancer. By the time they finished Year 12 the second crisis on Bougainville had escalated into a full-scale war as an uprising erupted against the government's efforts to reopen the notorious Panguna Mine.

One of the boys made up his mind to go and fight and as always his brother followed him without hesitation. They endured the harshest military training ever conducted by the PNGDF as the war was more dangerous than the previous conflict and found themselves deployed to the front lines after a few months.

In the Army they fought together side by side through the harsh weather and rainy nights in the deep Bougainvillean jungles that they patrolled with their unit. The sound of gunfire, men screaming in agony, illuminating flares and hand grenades brought hell upon them but they still fought with courage. Valour they showed, not for the sake of what was happening around them in the political scene but for each other and the brotherhood they had which required them to keep each other alive and safe. The two made a pact that if one of them was killed the other would bring him back home and not leave him behind on the front lines.

On a dark rainy morning their unit was called by headquarters to check out a small village high up in the mountains where military helicopters were attracting heavy machine gun fire from a group of rebels as they were evacuating wounded soldiers and villagers.

One of the boys was down heavily with malaria due to the heavy rains and was admitted to the base clinic. He was so sick he couldn't walk, the fever had brought him down to the point of seeing illusions created by his own mind; he was bedridden but was still eager to fight; not wanting to let his brother go out alone.

While he was sick in bed the unit was equipped and ready to leave. His friend came to the tent, held his hand and told him, "You're very sick, just take your medicine and stay put, wait till I come back, I promise that I will take you back home," After he reassured his friend he walked slowly out of the tent but heard his friend calling out, "Wait!" He came back to the bedside and his friend said, "Before you go please take this to keep you safe." The sick boy reached into his pocket and took out a necklace he had made from shells that they had found together on the beach while holidaying in his village. The other boy grasped the necklace and walked out of the tent to his unit which was waiting for him outside. The unit, fully equipped and battle-ready, began the long hike up the mountain through the heavy rain.

Two days went by and the unit didn't return. The heavy rain had cut off communications and no one knew where they were. The sick boy was worried about his friend; all sorts of thoughts converged on his mind. Is he safe? Is he still alive? Is he dead? All these questions drove him nearly to the point of insanity as his friend was closer to him than his own blood brothers.

With legs which wouldn't allow him to walk properly he looked at a childhood photograph of his friend and made up his mind that, no matter what, he had to go and find him. The malaria had badly affected him, he had lost a lot of weight and his legs and arms were very painful making it hard to walk and move.

The bond he had with his brother drove him to undertake an insane move. Without his commanding officer's consent he put on his boots, loaded his tactical bag with supplies and ammunition and smuggled an M16 assault rifle from the camp. He was determined to find his brother. When the sky went dark he covered up with a poncho and with his loaded gun slowly set off up the mountain under the intense downpour.

The rain showed no mercy and one could tell it wasn't going to stop. The boy was alone and still sick to the brink but no matter the weather or the constant threat of being shot or tortured by the rebels his spirit was not deterred from finding his friend. He hiked up the slippery mountain track for hours, dodging rebel patrols and with the fear of being bitten by snakes increasing as he ventured deeper into the bush. After the brutal hike a sigh of relief came out of his mouth.

On top of the mountain he saw a small hut. He went inside with his gun ready to take out anything that moved. The hut was abandoned so he decided to camp there for the night. In the hut as he sat by a small fire he heard the call of birds and his mind went back to his childhood days with his friend playing around on the street. He slept. Suddenly the cry of another bird woke him up. At that moment the rain had paused for a while as the sun came up. There was a whisper coming from the grass beyond the hut, calling his name.

The boy took his rifle and came out of the hut and crouched in the grass to hide from any enemy combatants. He crawled into the grass and saw a piece of camouflage cloth in front of him. It was the same material as the PNGDF jungle issue uniform. He kept moving as the voice echoed louder until he came to a clearing. As he emerged from the tall grass the boy went down on his knees and wept like never before.

In the clearing was the body of his dead brother, beaten up and bruised with two bullet wounds in his chest. Although he had endured the battle with the rebels and had been shot and died he had still managed to clutch tightly the shell necklace that his best friend had given him for luck. His friend went down on his knees and grabbed the lifeless body with tears streaming down his face. The person he knew and loved and always had at his back was gone forever.

A few days later he came back to Port Moresby filled with torment and a wounded heart. Instead of coming out of the aircraft with his brother at his side as before, he came out clutching the necklace in his palm accompanying the body of his fallen comrade and best friend wrapped in a PNG flag. Although he had lost the person he had kept near to his heart through the years he smiled bitterly as he had fulfilled the pact he made with him, his best friend who he called his brother until the end.

My Value, My Worth
Pamela Josephine Toliman

To my family and those who have gladly "eaten from my skin"
(kaikai long skin bilong mi):

Did you not see how I hung my head in embarrassment when you happily announced to the village that I had begun menstruating? You dressed me in magnificent plumes and soft fur. You oiled my skin and sang over me but I felt like a pig being groomed for exhibition.

"She is worth ..." you announced what I would be expected for my bride price as I was led forth and presented no longer as a child but a woman. From that moment I learnt a painful truth: I would never be my own and my value, my worth, would be dictated by others.

You considered my education an expensive luxury. Cleaning the house, fetching water and firewood, cooking and watching over siblings were things you pushed on me in an effort to increase my value. "No husband wants a woman who cannot cook or keep a home."

The increase in my domesticity value came at the price of missing out on a placement after grade ten. You were relieved that you would not have to waste any more money on school fees. Perhaps now you would see a return on your investment.

You would shamelessly appraise possible suitors in my presence. The fact that some candidates were already married or had fathered children was not considered impediments. Finally, one persistent suitor caught your attention and appetite. He began calling regularly at our home and you showered him with respect because of the money and gifts that accompanied his visits. Did you not see how he repulsed me? Did you not sense how sick I felt when his eyes roamed over my body?

You pushed me that day to accompany him into town. He had generously offered to advance you store goods for a small canteen I was to keep. You pushed me to accept his invitation. But he did not take me directly into town. He stopped at a quietly concealed garden house within his coffee plot. That day he took the last thing that was mine. Without my permission, he took and took again. I was battered, bruised and bleeding but nonchalantly he continued into town and bought me a Coke and a lunch pack to soften the blow.

I sat numb and silent as we waited for workers to load the store goods onto his vehicle. Finally we headed back and as our family home came into view hot tears burst forth from my eyes. Surely I was safe now? Surely you would not permit this man to ever come near me again?

When his vehicle pulled up, you happily greeted us and then called for tea to be brought for him. In the excitement of unloading the store goods you did not see me wince as I got out of the vehicle. You took no notice of how I walked stiffly into the house.

Later, when he had finally gone and after I had attempted to ease the discomfort of my torn flesh with water heated over the fire, I spoke to you of my ordeal. But the impression on your face churned what little there was in my stomach. You did not appeal to God or to justice, you appealed to the value of the store goods this man had delivered to your doorstep. "Look at how much he has given us!" You pleaded for me to take him as a husband; my ruin dismissed by store goods that were only valuable within their expiry dates. Again, you dictated to me my value, my worth.

Then you went about your polite demand for compensation and bride price. Did you not think to ask whether I wanted to be married to that man? As you anticipated, he paid for what he had already taken and would continue to take by force every time he wanted to be with me.

All that you had ever hoped to receive for my "skin" was laid at your feet on the day of my bride price payment; live pigs, live goats, cartons of lamb and mutton, store goods, garden food and cash to sweeten it all. The "eating from my skin" reached its climax that day.

You told me how proud you were of me for bringing in such a valuable haul. You told me that no other girl in our family had achieved such a feat. The prized pig had now earned her keep. She had been sold, not to the highest bidder, but to a monster that first stole then later paid.

Now my dear family and those who have gladly "eaten from my skin", I would like to set the record straight regarding my value, my worth: 800 kina* and not a toea more. This should cover the cost of an inexpensive plywood coffin, a white *meriblaus, a laplap* and a set of bed sheets. I have not included the value of tea, sugar and other items for the *hauskrai* because strictly speaking those things have nothing to do with my value, my worth but rather the size of your appetites.

The approximate value of a medium-sized pig in the PNG highlands is 800 kina. A pig of this size is suitable for cultural exchanges that occur during bride price payments, compensations and funerals.

A Dream Fades in the Sight of a Blind Love
Martinez Wasuak

Mablerose Kossigles had two elder brothers. She was beautiful and admired by many young boys in Maprik town west of Wewak. Mablerose was the daughter of a peanut farmer and they lived in the countryside. She was always advised by her two brothers and parents to have a happy marriage in the future and not to end up with an unwanted pregnancy or with a broken marriage.

At age 17 Mablerose did not continue her education after grade 10 but decided to seek employment to earn some money so that she could later continue her studies at Maprik Secondary School. She had always wanted to be self-reliant by funding her own school fees.

Because of her beauty, Mablerose was employed in a small hair salon in Maprik town, about a 20 minute walk from her countryside home. All the other young ladies who worked there were friendly and charming to Mablerose and she really enjoyed working with them. She was easy going and into sports and parties and because of her natural beauty she was not only admired by the employees in the hair salon but also by whoever she passed on the road or elsewhere.

One morning Mablerose was outside the salon and she was surprised to be given an invitation to meet someone in a nearby restaurant at lunchtime. The young woman who gave her the invitation didn't know who the fellow was who had asked her to deliver his letter. The letter only gave a description of the clothes that the writer was going to wear.

At first Mablerose was surprised and panicky but she was eager to find out who the person was. At lunch time she walked into the restaurant and positioned herself at the far end to see who would be coming to meet her. To her surprise, a young and handsome guy walked towards her and quickly introduced himself and ordered some food, which was brought to the table by an old lady.

While eating, Mablerose asked about him and he said his name was Lista Vermout. He continued telling her that he was a teller in the bank near the hair salon where she worked. He said he used to admire her because she looked prettier than all the other ladies. He said he couldn't hold back on his crush for her so he sent the invitation for them to meet so he could tell her in person what she meant to him.

Before he finished talking, she gave a little smile and dropped her eyes and nodded accepting his love and admiration her. The atmosphere around them at that moment was one of excitement for their new romance.

As weeks and months passed by they met regularly for lunch and romantic outings, whether a sporting event or a party. Their frequent meetings distracted Mablerose from her employment. She also seemed to forget all the significant advice from her brothers and loving parents. She no longer had time for those precious moments with her brothers and parents for advice and encouragement like before. All her free time was dedicated to Lista to walk by his side, hand in hand. Their friendship went well and Mablerose loved Lista very much for he was her first love.

One sad morning Mablerose received a letter from Lista saying that he had gone to Port Moresby and would call her later when he got settled. Mablerose couldn't believe he hadn't told here and her heart sank as the hot tears rolled down her cheeks. She left work and went home crying.

She waited for Lista to call but he did not. From that moment on she experienced sleepless nights with a wet pillow. She started to grow pale and thin as each new day came. With regret, and acknowledging the important advice that came continuously from her immediate family but which she had ignored, she shyly told her parents and brothers that she was pregnant with a child growing inside her.

Her elder brothers were angry, they got Mablerose's belongings and threw them out of the house and told her they didn't want to see her face again. They said that if they happened to see her around they would murder her.

With a broken heart and with great regret Mablerose took her belongings and went to Wewak and bought an Air Niugini ticket with the money she had earned from working to follow Lista to Port Moresby. There she rented a room at the Boroko Lodge for a week so she could look for Lista.

Mablerose started her search for Lista by checking the banks in the city in case he had transferred there from the bank in Maprik. With no sign of him, Mablerose walked slowly around the crowded city and looked at every man she came across to see if she could see Lista.

With the feeling of loneliness, hatred and love Mablerose toured all the streets of Port Moresby to find the man who had once fallen in love with her beauty and was the father of her unborn baby. But as each day passed she only saw strangers and not the one that she thought she loved and was longing to meet so that she could tell him she was pregnant.

She was really torn her apart and felt like falling down and dying. She felt that the world had turned its back on her and what she had to say would fall on deaf ears. All those feelings and conflicts made her burst into tears as she walked hurriedly to continue her search. With no one dear to ask her why she was crying or to comfort her she swallowed her tears and kept searching.

On the last day in the room that she rented in the lodge she really hoped that on that day she would be lucky and see him so she could go and live with him.

She was standing near a snack bar breathing in the

delicious aroma of food coming when she spotted Lista. He was walking with another lady as he passed her by. Mablerose called out Lista's name and he turned and saw Mablerose. But he walked away with the lady pretending he didn't know her. With a regretful feeling and anger burning inside her Mablerose stood helplessly watching them walking happily close to each other and out of her sight.

She boarded a plane the next day and went back home. When she arrived in Wewak town she hopped on a truck and went straight to the village house in Maprik. Her elder brother was chopping wood and without asking her to sit down or have a cup of fresh water he ran towards her with a piece of firewood. Before he could hit her she pulled a knife from her gwugewut and telling her brother she regretted what she have done in loving so blindly she pushed the knife straight into her own heart.

Gwuewut is a bilum from Nymikum village near Maprik with a pattern that symbolizes the waves a snake that lives in the water makes when it swims.

Lost in transition
Tanya Zeriga-Alone

Sitting by the fire at dusk, he looks like how any other old man would look - slumped over his betel nut *bilum*, waiting patiently for the womenfolk to bring his dinner.

The village people however, knew nobody would bring Eware his dinner. Whenever Eware ate, it was a necessity to keep from starving and not because it was the ritual mealtime.

Lately when Eware assumed this posture, his mind was miles away from his body, and his heart heavy within his chest. Old men are not supposed to cry but lately sorrow had become a constant companion. If you look close enough, you can see a path sculpted on his face by tears – tears, not even manly characters of stoicism and poise, taught to him in his youth could hold back.

It was a long time ago when he had a decent conversation with another adult human being. The last one was with his third wife before she disowned him just as the rest of the village did. No love lost. It was a marriage of convenience that served its purpose.

His first marriage was an arranged marriage for strategic purpose – his mothers' clan was running out of land to make gardens, so his marriage back into his fathers' clan was to facilitate access to land. Eware was eligible for marriage at 17 years of age.

The virtues of a woman were in how hard she worked and in the many children she could bear. Unfortunately, she was unable to give Eware any children after five years, which would continue facilitating his mother's clan access to garden land, so Eware and his family had to send her back to her father's house.

Eware took his second wife, a distant cousin to his first wife. Marriages had utilitarian value and physical attractiveness was a low priority. Over time, Eware grew fond of his wife despite her short stature and a limp from some childhood disease.

On his 15th year of marriage, his second wife died after a bloody and painful ordeal of birthing his fifth offspring – a breech birth. Through his children, Eware had secured access to garden land, but lost the person who would tend his gardens to feed his pigs which would be used to buy wives for his sons who would give him many grandchildren.

After the loss of his beloved second wife – the sight of his four bedraggled offspring all gathered around him for comfort was the energy he needed to be strong and revive the will to live. That was when he married his third wife for the convenience of his children. Even with a third wife, Eware pitched in more effort to looking after his boys than his third wife.

When the boys were younger, they had listened to him and stayed close to him. He looked after them the best he could, the way his father had brought him up. But boys grow up to be teenagers and eventually adults.

As his boys were growing up, the opportunity for a modern education became available. Eware had never seen the inside of a classroom in his days, but seeing the benefits of a modern education, Eware was determined that his sons would take advantage of the opportunities. He used his hunting skills to trap cuscus and wild pigs which he sold for money, and that was how he put his boys to school.

Johnny was the first born, he ran away from school when he was in grade six, because he disliked being made to sit still for long hours and for being rapped on the knuckles for practicing his English skills on his classmate. He could not understand why he has reprimanded because his teacher said it all the time – surely there was nothing wrong with saying "stupid bush kanaka". He was 18 years old then.

Johnny did eventually get a job at the nursery in town. His days filled with sieving soil and filling the black polybags for the local forestry project. That was where the rest of his brothers left their father to join him. Johnny, to his brothers' village eyes – was an epitome of a towner.

Things had not gone well for Eware when he sent his sons to school. He had compromised a cultural education for a modern education. The boys' time was occupied with gaining a modern education and that left no time for a cultural initiation. The latter was the bridge between a boy and boyish ways and a man with man responsibilities. Without this, his sons grew up not knowing their role in the family and in the village.

In his younger days, Eware had helped his father when his father needed him. Together with his two brothers, they had rallied behind their father to build his house, fight his battles and showcase the clan expertise.

Life, back in the old days was all about maintaining the family unit, and then as a family, contribute to the clan. Each clan had an expertise and therefore the strength of the tribe was in the strength of the clans to contribute their various expertise to maintaining the tribe. Eware's clan were great hunters and sons were gold; and Eware had hit the jackpot with four sons.

That afternoon like every other, Eware sat and imagined what it could have been if things were different, if he had insisted on initiating his sons instead of sending them to school. It was a risk he took. He risked the loss of culture for a better future where education meant money to buy his dreams and status. Without role models, his sons did not amount to any greatness in the education system. Similarly, the loss of a cultural education was huge.

Not knowing their place in the village the boys had moved to town to be with their elder brother. They had not learnt how to build a house, let alone court a girl in the culturally appropriate way. But the biggest regret for Eware was that none of his sons would know how to hunt. And his biggest shame would be when no sons stand beside him in the tribal council. None of them would be summoned for greatness when the clans gathered together to showcase their strength. He had taken a risk and lost the gamble both with the modern education system and the ways of his fathers.

He had also let Johnny go past the marriageable age because he had no money and pigs to buy his son a wife. If Johnny had stayed in the village, his brothers would have stayed with him. If only his wife had borne him daughters, the daughters would have brought him wealth through their bride price, and they would have looked after him into his old age. Daughters would also look after his pigs to buy brides for his sons.

He was an old man now, his muscles stripped of their vigor, his bones made brittle and crooked with age. His blood reluctantly propelled from a worn-out heart and his eyes losing the battle with cataracts. What could he do to turn back time, when time was running out on him? Even his last hope – his faith - was hanging by a thin thread between earth and heaven.

Eware was confused as to why his prayers to Anutu, this new God of love and mercy never went answered. He had followed all the rules to be loyal to this new sensation but despite his efforts, it seemed too hard to find favour in God's eyes.

It was a loss, felt right to the core of his bones when he let go of that little parcel containing a piece of bone and some hair – hunting magic, passed on from his father - when everyone in the village threw theirs into the bonfire to renounce their allegiance to culture and pledge their commitment to the local church. But it was for a better life, filled with milk and honey, he was told. No-one in the village knew what milk and honey was, but they all desired the clause about a "better life."

However, his ongoing struggles in life testified that his sacrifice was not enough. Sometimes, he wondered if maybe his inability to read the bible – printed in *tok pisin*, disqualified him from having fruitful audience with Jesus and his two counterparts.

With a heavy heart, he stared into the dying embers of the fire – lost in his thought until the cold began to seep into his bones. In automated movements, he crawled away from the fire to his corner and unrolled his sleeping mat and got ready to be tortured by another sleepless night.

POETRY

Melanesian Woman
Jessica Dobb

Brown smooth skin, tanned by the sun.
Black, brown eyes, blue by none.
A dancing smile with stained teeth.
No way near shoes or boots, she has strong feet.
Frizzy hair with coconut oil.
Tied to the back or combed out tall.
Baskets and *bilums* are her pride,
in *meri* blouses she will stride.
Down to the river or up to the hill,
with pots clanging her feet will drill.
A friend to many and mother to all,
despite her struggles,
she stands up tall.

A soliloquy of soil
Michael Dom

"What is the nature of soil?" I wondered.
"Soil is filthy and weak", a rock sneered at the earth
around it.
In a ploughed field I saw rocks crumbled to dust, where
my workers were hand tilling, and many more were piled
along the foot deep drains and at the head of each of a
score of forty metre long furrows.
"Now we can plant", I said.
This is the nature of soil.

"What is the value of soil?" I mused.
"Crops need top soil, but we grow anywhere", jeered some
weeds, rooted in deeply.

At noon my workers and I rested under the Tulip shade,
where we ate lunch and drank our fill of water, while
enjoying the cool wind that made the piles of cleared
debris burn more ferociously on our field.
"Return the ashes to the earth", I said.
This is the value of soil.

"What is the need of soil?" I thought.
"In 'Rainy Lae', almost anything can grow", echoed my
bedroom walls.
That night I dreamt of my mum's small backyard garden at
Fort Banner, where together we toiled, and how we shared
our harvest with neighbours, through the fence or over the
wall bordering our houses.
"This land is too dry, hard to dig and full of stones, but
you make magic Mrs Dom", they said.
This is the need of soil.

Sonnet 8: Dispela Nambawan Meri Tru
Michael Dom

Hamaspela gutpela man isave bihainim tok win bilong yu?
Hamaspela lidaman na hamaspela bikman tu?
Hamaspela man isave harim poret stori bilong yu?
Hamaspela man bilong tok singsing na hamaspela man
bilong Anutu?
Long wanem strong tru bai ol lusim naispela pasin bilong
yu?
Ol ino inap abrusim graun taim ol istap long lek bilong yu.

Hamaspela gutpela meri isave poretim tok win bilong yu?
Hamaspela bosmeri na hamaspela yangpela meri tu?
Hamaspela isave gut tru long bikpela bagarap bilong yu?
Hamaspela matron long haus sik na hamaspela meri bilong

Anutu?
Long wanem strong tru bai ol traim resis wantaim yu?
Ol ino inap abrusim dispela kalakala bilong yu.

Hamaspela meri na hamaspela man tru
Bai inapim mak bilong Dispela Nambawan Meri Tru?

Sonnet 8: The Perfect Woman

How many gentlemen have chased your myth?
How many captains and how many kings?
How many have heard of your legend fell?
How many poets and how many priests?
How could they resist your tender mercy?
They'll never deny the world at your feet.

How many gentle ladies dread your myth?
How many mistresses, how many maids?
How many have known your calamity?
How many nurses and how many nuns?
How, ever, could they dare compete with thee?
They'll never deny the world your beauty.

How many people, both women and men,
Meet the measure of The Perfect Woman?

Sonnet 12: A prayer for our times
Michael Dom

Above these trees towering
Above these deep blue seas
Above these clouds soaring
Above these mortal fears

Beyond these steep mountains
Beyond these battered slopes
Beyond these wasted plains
Beyond these shattered hopes

Through these shifting shadows
Through these darkening days
Through these shuttered windows
Through these dim lit doorways

Triune God, hear me pray
Let my people find their way.

Mo'anna
Alfred Eliesa Faiteli

In the pouring rain
Cross-legged she sat
Into the empty sky
Gazing!

Her eyes in emerald green
Her nerves draining lines of enmity
Her ebony hair
Soaked in silvery dew
Dripping!

Her naked body
Exposed
Radiating colours
Of a rainbow
Red green indigo
Blue violet yellow
Creamy dampish and cold
Shivering!

Her mighty lips
Distant and luring
Thick slippery velvety
And bubbling
Like when raindrops touch the sea
Soothing!

Her youthful pointed breasts
Tucked between her thighs
Tropical paradise
Untouched
Virgin
Where oceans mountains skies
Are almost
Touching!

She cuddled the misty air
Feeling romantic island fragrance
Frangipani leis
Marine-scented air
Tropical nostalgic aroma
Breathing!

In the rain showers she sat
Calm and still
Without company
Without romance
Without love
Yearning!

She turned
Waved
Smiling into my eyes
Tempting!

Can I resist?

No
I am coming…….
Oh! Mo'anna

It was on this island
Coral isolated faraway
I had this dream
In the pouring rain – wet

Drizzling!

A Cyclone is Coming
Alfred Eliesa Faiteli

The sky is so different
It's nothing like I've ever seen before
It's not the colours of the blue sea – waving in tides
Nor the colour of *niu* leaves – swaying in the sun
It's not the majestic colour of the silvery moon
Nor the splendour of the sinking sun
It is like that of a muddy puddle
When the murky bottom has been stirred
In this view
The sun hidden
Struggling to shine
Behind dark shadowy clouds
Racing past
A cyclone is coming

Strange it is
What we remember of our first love
I remember that storm
That drove you to shelter
In the cradle of my arms
I remember your velvety blouse
With three buttons undone

And the colour of your skin
I remember being held captive
By the scent of your floral perfume
And the look in your eyes
I remember being connected
To the beat of your heart
Lured by the softness of your voice
And the fragrance of love in your breath
That seduced my nostrils
A cyclone is coming

I remember
That time
We ran under the *udi* leaves
When the clouds opened
And the rain poured
When the horizon faded
And the winds pounded
When the tides changed
And the waves rose
When the thunder roared
And the lightning flashed
When the heavens closed
And the clouds opened
And it became dark
I knew
A cyclone is coming

I remember
That moment
How our lips met
Your arms slipping round my neck
My arms gripping round your waist
Tightly never to let go
When we discarded our *kalikos*
Shivering in cold
And took refuge

In our own bodies
When we made love
For the first time
Soaking in romance – wet
A cyclone is coming

I remember
Our wedding
On a sunny September day
In our local church down the road
A baby's cry echoed several years on
One......two......three......more cries
Breaking normal routine
Shortening nightly slumbers
Yet bringing joy in the morning
You managed well
Through all the stormy gale
Brewing in the air
A cyclone is coming

Now beside your bed I stand
Watching you sleep
A picture of serenity
Your hair falling – almost gone
Your dark purple lips – dry as dust
Your eyes – almost closing
Your body – thin and pale
Frail as you are
And in pain
Yet you smiled to me – gloriously
I stare into your face long and hard
And remember under the *udi* leaves
Thirty years ago
Drops of rain tick the windows
I look outside
And realise
A cyclone is coming

A salty tear rolls down my cheek
I quickly wipe away
Holding back the turmoil within
Fighting for life is futile
Like fighting a losing battle
Pain strikes me down into the visitor's chair
My tears stream like rain
My cries thunder in my ears
Waiting for only the doctor's answer
I knew
A cyclone is coming

Like petals of *siale* in the sun
The fragrance of your personality
Soon to fall and fade
I gape into my life-after
Empty hearted
Clutching your photograph to my heart
Its edges curled
Its luminance weak
But its image striking a thousand chords
Of love
Into my heart
Tomorrow will come another day
But your life
I will always cherish forever
Under the *udi* leaves – safe secure and sound

A cyclone is coming

Even a tomorrow got its own
Jeffrey Mane Febi

Heard the ticking of dawn
As with eyes without a lens I looked
Wrinkles of love lazily they pass by
Then Earth delivered and I was hooked
Hisses of storms old hastily rush by

Many a vivid plot pregnant with
Chances unaccounted for marched.
'Aaha heart', said I … 'look at you',
'Look at me … who between us'
'Is in greater pain … you knew!?'

Even a tomorrow got its own
Chances to be unaccounted for to moan
'Oh' said the heart. 'My joy isn't yours'
'And your pain is certainly yours'.

We don't sing anymore
Jeffrey Mane Febi

Here! Comfort and solace we seek. Where we love and
beloved.
Once a promise I smell; of together hearkening to sounds
of poetry;
Of to the beat of alliterations together dancing;
Of together in fields of metaphor, cuddling and be cheery;
Of through the bars of many a rhyme kissing.

Of a romance ever growing between us – you and I –
feeding on abstractions.
Words don't mean what they seem and substance of verses

reaches beyond yonder.
When ocean isn't deep, deeper we went; almost into bliss
and we did dance.
Pity! Our true love, how its symbols we do not have any
more I wonder.
Words mean what they seem and before yonder are our
verses' substance.

Dance I can't no more when there is no beat! But you
dance still,
Nor kiss you if there are no bars! But kiss oh kiss you will.
How I yearn you must know, for a return to the true ways,
Ever so close to the fields of metaphors – our true place.

Night Shift
Steve Ilave and Leonnie Paranda

Searching the night sky for my favourite star
Shifting through each twinkle near and far
Alas, she is not out there for me tonight
Why oh why are you out of sight?

Come out, shine bright
Make this heart light
Rouse this still night
Make this time right

Contemplating the heavens so vast
Wondering how long this predicament will last
Twinkle one more time that familiar flicker
Shine me a smile with that glorious glimmer

The night is no longer young
The night birds have all sung
Set at ease this anticipation
O heavens finest creation

Trillions of sparkles to tally
This forlorn gaze is wondering me silly
Hope's fading fast for you Twinkie
Could you like shoot by already?

Twinkie is there; somewhere
Keep looking and patience bare
It won't be long till the sky is kind
Twinkie's time is best; keep that in mind!

Dawns breaking perhaps tis time;
For her smile sublime
OMG, there YOU ARE
My Awesome Morning STAR!

Looked for her again this morning;
The clouds said: 'enough of this following'!
There is too much of this night-shift;
I'm sorry but I'm not going to lift'

But insistent I was
It was just because
Couldn't let clouds waiver
The hope that my day be better

And I must declare;
That the morning rays cannot compare!
To the feel of her soft touch at early dawn;
To the magic of the morning star I'll forever be drawn!

As a Writer
Diddie Kinamun Jackson

I sat and wrote and wrote
Into the moonlight
Upon the hard rock
Writing stories of the dream time
Stories passed down
And so old like time itself
Pondering hard into the dim firelight
Straining my mind
Just to write down everything
To preserve the story
As best I could

Chipping the cold hard rocks
Sweating into the cold chilly night
I gaze upon my scripts
Hands bleeding
From chipping to hard
Marvelling at the masterpiece
Created
I may be gone
But my story liveth
Upon this beautiful rocks
That bear my hands

Now I sit and write
Translating the beautiful scripts
On the ever now famous cave
Pen onto paper
I promise to write it down
As it is written
On the cold hard rocks

I write into the night
Under the low
Electric light bulb
The passion builds stronger
As each drop of ink
Touches paper
And the same old story
Becomes anew
In each breaking dawn

I write and write
Like my forefathers before me
My blood is the ink on my paper
It relates to my soul
And there is no end
To the words within
Wanting to be heard

I write and write
Hands getting tired
Mind growing weary
Not from exhaustion
But from every door
That closes in my face
I will not back down
It will not break my spirit
Nor weary my soul

I will write and write
Like those before me
Write as much as I can
Preserve as much as possible
Someday when I'm gone
The world will come to realise
We deserve to be heard

For this is no country
Without an identity
Written in a very beautiful story
Of how it is and
How it came to be
We deserve your attention.

The frustrating wait
Megghan Zeriga Jimbudo

You waited eagerly for them
standing on unwavering feet
casting nervous glances back and forth
you cannot wait any longer.

Your wait went unnoticed to them
they do not seem to mind
the eagerness in your mind is too much
are they pretending not to notice you?

Fighting unlimited thoughts on your mind
and with a heavy heart you trudge away
there is nothing you can do now.

Word has it that after you were gone
they seem to care and ask around for you
downcast you cannot wait any longer
frustrated you decided to move on.

The end
Mary Koisen

So it looks like it might be the end my Dear Love…
We're not fighting anymore.
I'm just not responding anymore.
I am not fighting to keep you anymore.
But I will not be the one to say "go, go out that door" as I
never have and nor will I ever.
The choice to go will be yours my Dear One
So that it wasn't said that it was I that sent you away my
darling love

My satisfaction will be that I tried and gave my all until I
gave out all my Dear Love
And in return I asked for the impossible and it got too
hard
And so the story will go
We wanted each other's love but at different stages in our
lives
I wanted what you've had but cannot have as long as I
continue to remain with you

So farewell my love my dear one.
I cannot let me go just to gain you…
Never mind, I'll find someone like you, and say adieu
As to sacrifice oneself, our beliefs, our concepts and
ideologies of love and happiness
We both know
Is a sacrifice we can't make…

The Rain Tree
Eric Kowa

On the edge of this blue marble
I hear echoes of a poacher's hammer, planting a rain tree
of steel and concrete
In a city with a new vision
Having felled trees of old, where life was worth life itself,
Where priceless was a rain drop, from nature's bosom,
trickling into streams of life
Where rivers used to sing with me, waltzing to the ocean

Oh you adulterous Nation! How long will you wander
Dancing under new reign - the money reign, waltzing to
the banks
Appetising a poacher's cocktail, of spiels and red beans
Just red beans

Oh Arise all you sons and daughters of the motherland
Lest you sleep now, only to wake in pool of beans,
Just red beans
In a rain tree of steel and concrete,
Where life, and all its promise, is nothing but plastic.

I am woman
Lapieh Landu

A poem inspired by the national Haus Krai. What does it mean to be a woman, a woman of the world and a woman of our country? What does it take to know our roles and to be respected for our role in society?

I am woman!
What does it mean?
To be woman.

My womb that cradled
A place for where he lay

My breasts, which fed my young
An ardour for my compeer

My hands, which served the needs of others
That prepares his repast for indulgence

My legs that stood so firm
As he lingered outside his abode

My face, hope for my emerging offspring
The reflection of his foundation

My voice, whispering words of wisdom
Comfort and alimony for his doubts

My spirit, the fireplace of our refuge
Gentle, benevolent and tenacious

I am woman!
This is what it means,
To be woman.

Koromira rises like the sun
Ishmael Palipal

As the wave crashes upon the seashore
the *pirites* sing morning greetings patrolling the shore
standing on Oema Bridge, watching the rising sun
across the horizon of the sea she raises, the old sun
every new day as a brand new day dawns,
I wondered why it rises up where it dawns

Every morning I love as her rays' touches me
I could stand there at it as it stares back at me
my place is Koromira where the sun rises
the eastern part of the *sankamap* islands
eastern shores of my beautiful Bougainville
That's is where the sun first saws her avail

As the darkness gives ways to red-orange colours
the sun paints the first skies with orange colours
I always watched as the painter paints the sun
the pretty rising big yellow round morning sun
the artist of the universe quickly changes colours
started with black to orange and yellow colours

So Koromira rise like the sun rises out of the sea
I want us to rise from the sea and look to see
to see the people staring back at my beauties'
want the world to see and say my wonders
Koromira the sun rises from your seas up
so why not new things rises from there up

As the sun renews her-self beneath the ocean
so do you be renewed under the crushing ocean
and give light and life starting from the lands
starting from where the sun is seen first on lands
reaching out to others as the sun's rays reach me
Koromira rise up like sun rays reaches to touch me

Koromira — the area of Central Bougainville where I come from
Pirites — dancing tail birds
Sankamap — sunrise.

Ballad of Meri Koromira
Ishmael Palipal

This girl of Koromira that he loves
she is pretty and lovely in her ways
her eyes blaze like the morning sun
and glows with a light of a skylight sun
her eyes are welcoming and resistible
This meri Koromira she is very adorable

Her lover said her body is so tender
it is a fine craftsmanship of the creator
the touch of her skin is a magic feeling
a feeling that can you send you off dreaming
of fantasy that she might be yours forever
to hold her tied in your hands wherever

Her body is shaped like that of a model
smoothly curved as a guitar model
finely shaped for the hands to fit hold
to cuddle her by her lover as she is hold
she loves her lover's touch like her lover
and he is everything she can image forever

Their love grows stronger as they discovered

things that are lovely and amazing but uncovered
lovers came closer and closer as they grow stronger
deeper and deeper they fall in love with their wonder
encouraging and discouraging alone the way to love
he said the journey is rough but the thing is love

The thing is love that drives him towards her
for her lips is sweet as the honey his sweet dear
the kiss that she breaths is unforgettable
for she is the one and only girl unspeakable
the naispela meri eastern coast side of Solomonia
the unforgettable woman the Meri Koromira

My Papua New Guinea
Marie-Rose Sau

Land of my heart
Birth land of my forefathers
The land surely cried blessing
And gave birth to a *mama graun*
Richer than all the silver and gold
Diamonds and crystals
And daring riches of all the worlds

Land of my heart
Tested and tried
Used and abused
To the very core
Still you stand proud
Still you give all that you can

Land of my heart
The perfect painting of paradise
Beautiful treasure
Buried among the atolls galore

Across the Pacific
Still you lie humbly in wake
My *asples*
Home to my ever worried heart

Land of my heart
Years on end
The music of my fathers have played
The sounds of the *kundu* beating

A stampede of human feet
Dancing to the rhythm
Voices ringing out
Days on end

Land of my heart
Tribesmen and tribeswomen
They chanted
Worshipped the land
The trees and birds
And they worship God
The Almighty God that made you
O land of my sighing heart

My now beautifully tragic land
The hardships you watched unfold
Yet you stand tall
And gave all

They called us cannibals
But were we really?
Home to my wondering pride
A land for evermore blessed than cursed
Land of my heart
For evermore my Papua New Guinea

A Faceless Silhouette
Pamela Josephine Toliman

*For the 'natives' who suffered and died at the hands of the Japanese
during World War II*

At the water's edge, a faceless silhouette points back to a
time when many stood alone, though surrounded and
cornered like prey.
At the hands of cruel oppressors they cried for mercy, they
begged for a better end.
No memory or monument exists for these people. Their
dark skin, further blackened by the tropical sun, pushed
them deep into the shadows of obscurity.
They now inhabit a place where the light of remembering
cannot reach them.
They remain nameless and faceless within their restless
sleep.

Embraced Through Éclairs
Emma Wakpi

It was a Tuesday evening
I remember well
Agnes, Gertrud and I
With Ruth around her table

After dinner conversations
Stories, memories and jokes
Then got talking about food
And I mentioned what I missed most

You see in PNG
Éclairs are hard to get

71

But they're my favourite sweets
And I lamented that fact

"*Was ist éclair*?" Ruth asked
The word was new to her
Agnes tried to explain
But seemed to get nowhere

Ruth sat there for a while
Then walked briskly to her kitchen
Where cook books were extracted
And for éclairs we were searching!

When finally shown the recipe
She said "*oh mi sori tru*"
With a sigh and a shrug
I replied "*yes, mi tu*"

"*Bai mi mekim b'long yu*"
Said Ruth her eyes taking on a gleam
Then with a grin began another conversation
Éclairs forgotten (or so it seemed)…

The next day was filled with activities
As holiday matters were pursued
Éclairs were totally forgotten
In the ensuing holiday mood

Then in the afternoon
When resting from a busy day
There's a knock at the door
And there's Joas with a tray!!

Éclairs! Éclairs! Éclairs!
They looked and smelled soooo good!!
I was overwhelmed
And prayed "Oh God bless Ruth!"

My heart was warmed
My taste buds delighted
I savoured every bite
And basked in what it represented

For in this generous gesture
God's love I saw, felt and tasted
His embrace conveyed through éclairs
Through Ruth's warm hearted present

Companion
Martinez Wasuak

*This poem is dedicated to my sister and friend, Verlyn Apis, on her
23rd birthday today*

Companion
Courageous and fun filling
You notice my weaknesses and sketch my strength
When you smile, I feel human and walk the path
Strength

Companion
Grows my bone
You tell me to avoid drugs and write me a balanced diet
When I sight you, it took all my depressed feelings
Guiding pearl

Companion
Took off the loneliness
You make melodies and keep my room ablaze
When you talk, it gives me peace and brings my family
closer
Union

Companion
Love and caring
You hope on the boat with me when I'm sailing the
stormy seas
When my golden day comes we share happiness
Legitimate comrade

The white man's materialism
Martinez Wasuak

Here, take my speed boat
Give me your wooden canoe
Here, take my steel axe
Give me your stone axe
Here, take my cash
Give me your *tapu*
Here, take my steel pot
Give me your clay pot

Here, take my jewelry
Give me your *kina* shell
Here, take my linen lap lap
Give me your grass skirt

Here, take my magneto
Give me your bamboo fire stick
Here, take my linen bag
Give me your feathery *bilum*

Here it's white's man materialism
That diminishes traditional lifestyle.

Tumbling Calamities
Ganjiki D Wayne

I can't get my head around all these
After a political coup we've had tumbling calamities
Controversy abounds, power-plays come faster
And we're rocked by disaster after another
We thought an SC decision will fix all, but PMNEC
happened
We tried to handle that, and the Governors General
happened
We tried to work that out, and the Police Commissioners
happened
We tried to deal with that, and the floods happened

We tried to deal with the floods, and the land slipped
We tried to handle the slip, and the soldiers mutinied
We tried to work out the mutiny, but the ship had sunk
We tried to focus on the ship, and the CJ ran out of luck!

Lord knows what'll happen next!
Just watch the phone we'll know by text
Facebook'll break to us the news
Some storm of late, shall again rock our shores

We blinked, and our nation's changed
Landscapes-political social physical-rearranged
At the snap of some fingers; but who's fingers?
Among the people it's mostly hurt that lingers

We asked for, no we demanded, change
But we didn't bargain for this kind
And now here we are lost and deranged
Angry, mad, demanding one's faulty behind

No time to grieve, not even to anger
No time to rejoice, pleasure none, no glee
Hurting and lost, forever confused
Take one week for yet another cuppa tea

Ol' Pete crowned himself at an opportune time
For in these calamities he can truly shine
But a cloud hovers o'er his head
A crisis that I pray soon be fixed
What our Mama Lo says bout him and that seat

Pray tell what becomes of us all!
Does nature unleash its disapproval?
Have our sins and our leaders' folly
Brought wrath on this nation wholly?

Reality Bites
Tanya Zeriga-Alone

Alas my rose coloured glass
Smashed into a thousand pieces
The thousand fragments scattered all over
No more Technicolor dreams
No more rainbow painted view
Just a darker shade of grey
Reality sure is stark
Alas my euphoric soul
Wrung dry of its living waters
No more butterfly swoops in the gut
No more adrenalin rushes and cascades
Only the upward surge of gall
Living the mouth burning
The foul breath lives to tell
Reality sure is bitter

Alas my bubble of dream
Popped in mid-air by invisible fingers
My fantasies hitched a ride with the passing wind
Leaving not a footprint neither a shadow
Not even a note
O clueless me
Tell me where has my dream gone?
To the wind - Please bring back my illusion

ESSAYS

The hypocrisy of mateship, fair go and human rights in Oz
Erasmus Baraniak

I have previously discussed and at length the merits of the Australian values of 'mateship' and 'fair go' from a Melanesian perspective.

I described their humble nautical origins and essential veracity from a convict mariner's perspective, and how then Prime Minister John Howard attempted to squeeze from the survival catchcries of convicts in cramped, crowded and disease infested convict ships, a set of values that would become the rite of passage for a modern state and its people.

What has become increasingly clear about these egalitarian notions of "mateship" and "fair go" is the underlying admission that everybody is not having a fair go in Australian post-convict society.

This is certainly true in the case of Aborigines, Torres Strait Islanders, refugees and other minority groups in terms of health, education, social services, social justice, criminal justice, human rights, and social equity. They are not treated like mates and accorded the basic minimum of a fair go.

Australia has one of the worst social justice and human rights records of any country in the developed world in its treatment of indigenous citizens, and the magnitude of oppression meted out to them is right up there with history's hand on Jews, Kurds, Armenians, Tibetans and, closer to home the East Timorese and West Papuans.

A dismal human rights record has been exacerbated by successive governments, both Liberal and Labor, who treat boat people cum refugees with contempt and brand them as "illegals".

The treatment meted out to boat people who are fleeing injustice and turmoil in their own countries is nothing short of criminal. I don't know of any instance in history where it has been made a criminal act for an individual or a family of oppressed persons, fleeing persecution, and in some cases possible death, to seek a better life in another land.

This is particularly so if, for instance, where these are people from war ravaged areas like Afghanistan, Iraq and Sri Lanka.

In the case of Afghanistan and Iraq, Australia parades itself as the liberator, a beacon of freedom, bringing the hope of democracy to these countries by waging war against them, ostensibly to liberate them.

In what appeared to be a noble quest, which started in Iraq, to rid the world of weapons of mass destruction, Australia is partly responsible for slaughtering, or causing to be slaughtered, half a million people in under ten years, bombed to rubble the cities and villages of Iraq and destroyed the way of life of millions.

The WMD basis for the invasion of Iraq has now been discredited as a huge lie perpetrated by the US government and its Coalition of the Willing (to lie and cover up). There were no WMDs, and the US knew this, but chose to lie to the whole world.

Bishop Desmond Tutu of South Africa recently announced he is prepared to sue, and put on trial, former US president George W Bush and former British Prime Minister Tony Blair for war crimes against the people of Iraq.

Bishop Tutu is taking issue with the US and UK governments because of the blatant lies they told the world to give them license to kill and destroy a nation. Bishop Tutu says that was absolutely un-Christian conduct on the part of the US and UK.

In Afghanistan, in a bid to rid the world of Talibanism Australia, has participated in the slaughtering of well over

300,000 people. The number of people slaughtered is increasing every day, and is justified on the basis of the Coalition partners wanting to give these people the noble and wonderful gift of democracy.

Looking at the number of deaths, you have to ask, is democracy so noble that it has to be paid for by the blood of innocent children, mothers, fathers and grandmothers?

When Afghan people flee their homes and turn up at the doorstep of Australia to be part of this democratic utopia, this paradise of freedom, they are either allowed to drown at sea or captured and imprisoned either in Australia or in some remote Pacific location such as Manus Island, where they will have no access to Australian media and Australian courts.

Even the once independent Australian media has been compromised. With the active encouragement of their government, the Australian media have joined the Canberra chorus, seeking to demonise genuine refugees by calling them illegals, queue-jumpers, or wealthy middle-class Arabs, Iraqis or Afghans bribing boat captains and crew in Indonesian ports to claw their way into Australia.

It is curious that, apart from the Aboriginal landowners of the Australian continent, the convict settlement of Australia was by people who arrived illegally and uninvited. They were the first boatpeople. They were the first illegals. They have no better standing or claim to Australia than others who came subsequently by boat.

Yet they seek to haul their offensive layers of lies and trickery before us in Melanesia, masquerading as just laws by a just government to give them dignity beyond their true status, all the while living off the fat of Aboriginal lands in the existing Aboriginal nations.

The slaughter of ancient Aboriginal nations, the shifting of tribes away from their homelands, the taking of children and the creation of internment camps were all organised by the British under what they believed to be correct legal premises.

Such premises never made allowance for the law of the land (Aboriginal law) to determine the rightness or wrongness of this trespass upon Australia.

It has been stated that this was the fundamental miscarriage of justice upon which Australian society was founded. To this day, without proper recognition of this wrong, without just and fair recompense to the Aboriginal tribes of Australia, the government and its institutions are based upon a felony. The very notion is a continuous act of criminality. White Australia has taken what the Aboriginal people never gave.

It is true that white Australia has not in recent times carried out raiding parties on Aboriginal communities with guns and bayonets as it did in the massacres of the late 1800s and early 1900s. It does not have to.

It has set up a system of government and welfare that annihilates a people just the same, a system that condemns indigenous people to illiteracy, poor health, substance abuse, dysfunctionalism, hopelessness, and gradual but certain death.

The current human rights record of Australia toward its indigenous people is such that there is very little hope in sight for these people who currently fall way below any internationally accepted standard and indicator.

Just go out to Alice Springs on a summer's night by the Todd River course and you will see played out before you this ritual of deprivation and subjugation that has become an acceptable way of life. Today, many groups are calling upon the Australian government to increase the dole so that people can simply afford a loaf of bread every day.

In the country town of Nowra, just south of Sydney, once bustling with orchards and dairy farms, there is a flood of indigenous former dwellers of inner city Redfern, forced from their place because Howard's Australia didn't want Olympic visitors to see indigenous people living in squalor in city slums.

They line up in the dole queues of dysfunctional Nowra, a town where you can even smell death and despair in the breeze knifing up Junction Street.

In Walgett, a country town in western New South Wales, there is 99% unemployment amongst indigenous people; many of them third, fourth and fifth generation indigenous unemployed.

They are mostly illiterate and given birth to children who form a whole new generation of dysfunctional and illiterate people, addicted to substances and subject to every other abuse imaginable.

Almost 95% percent of indigenous youth in Australia have little or no chance of advancement to university, nor completing high school. The healthcare and sanitation standards among indigenous Australians are third world and nothing like what most white folk take for granted.

For many remote indigenous communities around Australia a quick audit of basic human rights compliance will reveal that Australia, as a first world developed country, has failed miserably in its treatment of its black people.

Australian families in suburbia treat their pets better than their government treats the original landowners. This is a sad indictment on a country that is seeking to bring health, education, law and order, equal opportunity and rights advocacy to the Pacific.

It has no solid foundation to work from in terms of real successes with its own black people. Australia practices symbolism with indigenous people, but is not serious about addressing its own real injustices, discrimination, prejudice; inequality and race based social injustice.

Some 20 years ago, over 95 Aboriginal deaths in custody were reported by a Royal Commission of Inquiry. In each case it recommended the prosecution of members of the Police for causing the deaths. To this day not one single Australian policeman has been charged. That is hardly what one would call a fair go.

In the recent case of a Palm Island Aboriginal death in police custody, Cameron Doomadgee died of broken ribs and a torn liver within half an hour of being arrested. The Queensland Director of Public Prosecutions attributed the death to an "accidental fall" and concluded the police had no case to answer.

This decision was totally contrary to findings of a detailed coronial inquest that suggested foul play by Police. How does a person 'accidentally' die of four broken ribs, a ruptured portal vein, a liver almost cleaved in two, a black eye, bruising to the forehead and back of his head, bruising to the upper part of his back and on both his hands, all taking place in a police station where a very fit and disproportionately large policeman had earlier in as much as confessed to a 'fight' between himself and the deceased on a videotaped police interview?

The policeman, who had earlier confessed to falling on the victim, was later allowed to change his story to falling beside him.

How does a slightly built man, slightly inebriated but happy moments earlier, whistling and singing, 'accidentally fall' and sustain such a large number of injuries, most of which could not be sustained or explained either scientifically or clinically by a single fall from a stand up position?

The events and the incongruous findings smack of funny business in the Australian justice system and are well documented by Chloe Hooper in her book, *The Tall Man*.

The predominantly white police force in Queensland, as a sign of solidarity and mateship, threatened to boycott police services to Aboriginal communities in protest over the subsequent prosecution of the white Palm Island police officer.

What about the case of David Hicks, five year's incarceration without any charges in a foreign prison?

Hicks, an Australian who confessed to training with terrorists was allowed to languish in Guantanamo Bay by then Australian foreign minister, Alexander Downer, without any due process of law.

Nowhere in the case of Hicks were the spirit and values of "mateship" and a "fair go". Whatever happened to democracy and the law that requires a fair and speedy trial, let alone the presumption of innocence until proven guilty in a proper court system?

It was curious that most of the judges on the US Supreme Court appointed by successive Bush (father and son) administrations were disturbed enough to find it judicially profane to endorse the antics in Guantanamo.

If Australia believed in the rule of the law in a democracy, then the ruling of the US Supreme Court should have bothered both John Howard and Alexander Downer. .It obviously did not.

What is the content of 'fair go' and "mateship" in a modern democracy if it does not consist of due process for the likes of Hicks and the likes of boat people arriving on the shores of Australia?

What could possibly be at the heart of this generation of politicians, both Liberal and Labor, that compels them to instantly abandon the values of democracy, human rights and due process, let alone mateship and fair go, and summon such capacity for callous indifference?

What has become of the condition of man that he abandons his state of enlightenment, the gains of the last 200 years, and takes on the cloak of profanity, of a wayward and misguided being, and retraces his footsteps into that long forgotten darkness of the Stone Age and the Middle Ages from which we have evolved?

For the Pacific countries, especially the Melanesian States, Australia's human rights record and its treatment of its indigenous people is a measuring stick for realising that no matter how much money Australia spends on the Pacific, it has no real values to guide it as a nation.

It has had little or no practical or policy success in dealing with its indigenous people, especially in education, health, economic advancement, social justice and equality.

If Australia does not understand and care for its own indigenous people, with successful and humane policies that work, how can the Pacific people, especially Melanesians, expect that anything good will come out of Canberra, in particular for Melanesian people?

How can Melanesians trust a white Australian government that does not deal fairly and equitably with its own black people?

How can Melanesian landowners and resource owners trust Australian companies and the Australian government who have stripped the black people of Australia of their lands, their resources and their way of life?

How can we trust a nation of people with no values, whose only affinity is to dollars and cents?

Belden Namah's prison dreams: a couple of steps to go
Kela Kapkora Sil Bolkin

The Sandline International mercenaries arrived in Papua New Guinea in February 1997. Brigadier-General Jerry Singirok, the army chief, denounced the Sandline deal and called on Sir Julius Chan to resign. So Sir Julius sacked him.

But the PNG Defence Force refused to cooperate with his replacement. Brigadier-General Singirok retained the support of the 4,700 members of PNG's army.

All these events unfolded when I was a first year student at the University of Papua New Guinea.

The PNGDF soldiers made a new home at the university's Forum Square. The university students and the soldiers unanimously opposed Sir Julius hiring the mercenaries to flush out the Bougainville Revolutionary Army.

The police force was true to its constitutional duty and tried its best to protect the lives of civilians as well as public property and assets. But there were a couple of instances where the police and the defence force soldiers came close to firing shots at each other.

At the beginning of their protest, the students and the soldiers shared food from the university mess. This show of solidarity and camaraderie was consistent with the traditional PNG way of preparing for tribal warfare.

There were five defence force officers heading the protest: Major Walter Enuma; Captain Bola Renagi; Captain Belden Namah; Lieutenant Michael David; and Second Lieutenant Linus Osaba.

These soldiers played a crucial role in stopping the mercenaries from going to Bougainville to kill and murder the BRA fighters.

Every time Namah took the podium in his full military regalia to deliver a speech he looked like the Napoleon Bonaparte that we had read about in history books.

He could truly talk and had the students, the soldiers and everyone standing on their toes with their adrenaline soaring.

That was the first time I had heard and seen Namah, albeit from a distance. At the time I didn't realise he would end up where he is now.

Civilians living in the various settlements in Port Moresby inundated the Waigani campus to show their support for the students and soldiers.

A couple of government vehicles were stolen and driven into Forum Square and burnt as a warning to the Chan-Haiveta government about what to expect if they sent the mercenaries to Bougainville.

Over the next two or three days the student leaders used rhetoric and demagogy to maintain the momentum of the protest.

Some dissenting students who claimed that the leaders were using the crisis for their own means were harassed. So were students who didn't get involved in the protest and tried to attend normal classes.

Fearing intimidation, they refrained from school work and sat at Forum Square listening to the student leaders talking about Tiananmen Square and the liberation movements in Latin America and Africa.

People like Fidel Castro, Che Ernesto Guevara, Nelson Mandela, Hugo Chavez and other revolutionaries were hailed and used as examples of the approach needed in the crisis.

Few of the civilians, students and soldiers had an understanding of the nature and rationale of the deal signed by the Chan-Haiveta government with Tim Spicer of Sandline International. They only had the opportunity to hear the side of the story espoused at the UPNG Forum Square.

The two daily newspapers were burnt or destroyed if they reported on the advantages of the deal to have the mercenaries eliminate the BRA.

The organisation Melanesian Solidarity (MelSol) was part and parcel of the protest and was very vocal. Jonathan Baure, Peti Lafanama and Powes Parkop were some of the leaders of MelSol and made names for themselves during the crisis. Some student leaders like Tom Olga and David Arore also became well known because of the crisis.

In the 1997 national general election many of the MelSol and student leaders stood for election in their various provinces. They thought that they had made themselves popular enough during the crisis to get elected.

But in the end only one of them, Peti Lafanama, was successful and joined the other new faces, like the late Fr Robert Lak, in parliament.

During the protest, students, soldiers and the general public, and various opportunists, slept outside both the northern and southern gates of National Parliament demanding that the Chan-Haiveta government tear up the deal with Sandline International.

Eventually the 40 Sandline mercenaries were sent packing from Port Moresby and never set foot in Bougainville nor fired a shot there.

Sir Julius Chan resigned on 26 March 1997 taking with him his deputy, Haiveta, and defence minister.

After the crisis, the law took its course. Namah was tried for mutiny, convicted and gaoled in late 1997 with all his fellow officers except Major Walter Enuma. Namah was locked away, nobody heard of him again and he seemed to have faded into the abyss of history.

Around 11 September 2001 when the Islamic militant group al-Qaeda hijacked four passenger jets and crashed them into the World Trade Centre and the Pentagon, I was granted permission by the then CIS Commissioner Richard Sikani to carry out a 10-week research program looking into prison rehabilitation at Bomana gaol.

I entered the main Bomana compound and met Namah at the entrance to the European area. He was clean shaven and wore short dark sportswear without a shirt.

He introduced himself and it quickly dawned on me that he was one of the soldiers that had led the Sandline protest. He was living in the European compound with a couple of the other officers implicated in the mutiny.

There were also a couple of policemen, a Fijian and two Chinese who had been involved in various crimes ranging from murder to felony. Namah was very obviously the leader among the prisoners in the European compound and he had secured a freezer, decent beds and a TV for his fellow inmates.

For the next 10 weeks, Namah and I met at the Bomana main compound library for lunch. Whilst munching on our brown rice and tinned fish we discussed socio-economic and political issues affecting Papua New Guinea.

Through our discussions, I came to realise that he knew all the factions in the PNG Defence Force and which politicians they were affiliated with. He was also aware of all the major white collar crimes and embezzlement taking place from the public coffers and would strenuously condemn these crimes.

"This country is a land of milk and honey and I want to become the prime minister one day and save this country from both illegal and legal exploitation of our wealth and diversity.

"We are too polite to foreigners and that in itself is setting ourselves up for ambush by greedy foreign corporate organizations who are obsessed with profits, cheap labour and compliant markets. PNG's interest is the last thing on their priority list,' Namah said.

I listened attentively but at the back of my mind I was wondering how a helpless prisoner could get out of prison and give birth to his dreams and aspirations.

We became well acquainted and every time I went to the main compound he greeted me as '*Angra*'.

I tell you, Namah can talk and talk on any issue with vigour and conviction.

Every week when I entered the Bomana CIS I brought the two daily newspapers for Namah to read. He would read through them making comments on all the political rhetoric and grandstanding by politicians and corporate organisations.

He had an opinion on how it could all be done better with less cost, or no cost, to catalyse hugely successful results and impacts.

I was impressed with his ideas but deep down in the bottom of my heart I was underestimating him and was sure that he would die without realising his dreams, not least because of his prisoner status.

Then in 2003 the news was splashed on the front page of both dailies that Namah had been granted parole for his part in the Sandline Crisis. He quietly returned to his Bewani Forest like Robin Hood did to Sherwood Forest in English folklore.

I don't know what he did between 2003 and the eve of the 2007 national general elections.

In 2007 he stood for the Vanimo Green River Open seat and won. He returned to tackle his arch enemies at the Waigani *Haus Tambaran* (Parliament) and the Galleries of Justice.

From that point on, all is familiar and we all know he helped oust Sir Michael Somare's nine-year old government and install Peter O'Neill as prime minister. He landed in the deputy prime minister's seat.

With the connections he had, he cooled and contained the mutiny by Defence Force soldiers supporting Somare. He also combed the Supreme Court building looking for the chief justice.

If Namah is still the same guy that I became acquainted with at the Bomana prison in 2001 then I feel that one day he will climb the remaining couple of stairs to reach the apex.

I also believe that his prison dream of becoming prime minister one day will also unfold.

You and I know that PNG is the land of the unexpected. Let us wait and see if this prophecy of mine becomes reality.

We all know the adage, 'Where there is the will, there is the way'. It is also useful to remember that other adage, 'All great visions are reached in stages.'

Wahgi Hellcats: a rock band 'born before its time'
Kela Kapkora Sil Bolkin

The Wahgi Hellcats was a famous rock band in the Papua New Guinea music industry well before the Australian flag was lowered in 1975.

The band was humbly born in the Minj area of the Jiwaka Province in December 1973. The founder was a self-taught musician who started with a ukulele in 1963.

Pat Siwi (pictured) was only 18 years old when he started the band and since then he has become a household name.

He is now among PNG's top music icons, just like the late John Wong, George Telek and Henry Peni. His Wahgi Hellcats also sits comfortably among other top bands like Barike, Painim Wok, April Sun and Sirosis.

In the 1960s, young Pat had a very close friend, David Peri, who was a half caste Simbu-Sepik.

Pat and David attended Minj primary school and soon realized they both liked music. At the same time, they found one of Pat Siwi's cousins, Siwi Muruk, who was also half caste Simbu-Sepik and who also liked music.

Pat, David and Siwi officially came together and formed a band in December 1973. They named it the Wahgi Hellcats.

In those nostalgic days Pat was the main vocalist and played guitar. David was the harmonist and played bass guitar. Siwi had the drums perfectly under control.

They started playing around clubs using borrowed instruments. Most of the equipment was borrowed from the University of Technology where Pat was an architecture student from 1971 to 1973.

Since the birth of the Wahgi Hellcats many other musicians have come and gone, but the band has satisfied the test of time.

Siwi Muruk was a bit of a humbug and Pat had to keep an eye on him all the time. Fortunately, Pat was a natural leader and he kept the group together and the legacy they left in the highlands and the PNG music industry stands head to head with other consistent performers like Barike, Painim Wok, April Sun and Sirosis.

Pat Siwi's leadership abilities were not a fluke. He is from the Enduga tribe of the Simbu Province and his mother is from Enga. Pat's mother is from the first sister; Peter Ipatas, the proactive and popular veteran Enga Governor, is from the second sister. And Daniel Kapi, a former MP, is from the third sister.

"I thought I was born before my time. There was no music industry in PNG when I started," said Pat.

I probed him about the song *New York City* and he said Tony Cristi, an American friend, gave him the lyrics. "Cristi and I composed the song only to test our market value abroad," said Pat.

Years later, the younger generation spread a rumour that the Wahgi Hellcats band was heading to New York and had composed the song on the way. "I've never been to the US so it is a lie," he said.

Pat did his last live performance in 1988 and then settled down to build a recording studio. In 1991 he launched the Kumul studio in Goroka and started recording a few of the individual musicians and bands throughout the country.

Then around 1999, with DJs, DVDs, CD burners and discos proliferating, he knew the studio was not going to make money. The devaluation of the kina also reduced his profit margin so he closed Kumul studio. His competitor, Pacific Gold Studio, shut its doors at about the same time for the same reason.

"Anyhow, I am still doing music to raise money, especially for charity. I flew down from Goroka to play at the Crown Plaza to raise funds for Team Simbu to travel to East New Britain for the PNG Games," Pat said when I met him outside the Papuan Rugby league club house that evening as he was on his way to the Crown Plaza to do a live performance.

The tickets were sold for K500 per person and that night alone they raised more than K114,000 for Team Simbu.

December 2013 will mark the 40th anniversary of the Wahgi Hellcats band and Pat Siwi and its members are planning to release an anniversary album. All the songs will be in English. They will also travel to the major cities in PNG for live grand performances.

Pat Siwi has a different view of Chin H Min's current promotion of PNG musicians through the EMTV *Mekim Music* shows. He prefers more live performances from PNG musicians. According to Pat live performances are real music. What we see on EMTV is 'lip sinc' - miming.

"For all musicians, their real worth and expertise is tested during live performances. At the moment they look great on TV but unfortunately they don't give the fans the same taste and feel that you get with the manoeuvres during a live performance.

"Furthermore, the musicians at the end of the TV shows go back to the ghettos and live in rags. It is a fraud." Pat is adamant that PNG musicians should step up and make more money from live performances.

Pat Siwi is not confident about the future of the PNG music industry and has called for government intervention by way of legislation and policies. He thinks the Institute of PNG Studies should expand beyond recording traditional songs to also house and coordinate the contemporary PNG music industry.

"In that way, the music industry can also have technical management capacity to formulate policies to contain the threat of music piracy and blue toothing.

"Then again, even if we make laws, who will enforce them?" he asks. "The answer to this could put off potential young musicians who wish to ply their trade. It is a wedge that has splintered the PNG music industry into shambles and chaos."

Pat agrees with Markham Galut, Ratoos Gary, Tony Subam and Pius Wasi - who are also top Papua New Guinean musicians, dancers, actors and comedians - that PNG artists need to produce music using more traditional sounds to break into the international market.

The contemporary PNG artists according to these veterans are all 'copycats' and using too much rap.

Pat Siwi laments that he has met a top PNG musician lately who moaned that he could not make money like he used to before due to piracy and blue toothing. Should musicians who want to make money have to move out of PNG and increase live performances, he wonders.

In the meantime, the fans of Wahgi Hellcats band should start saving their money to purchase the 40th anniversary album come December 2013. Surely there will be live performances too.

I feel that Pat is absolutely overdue for a knighthood from the Queen of England or a Logohu award from the fat cats.

PNG has a tradition of awarding the Queen's honours and Logohu awards to club boys and pedestal leaders.

Pat is truly a servant leader who has contributed immensely to music over almost four decades. Hence, it is only fitting for Pat Siwi to be honoured by *Misis* Queen, just like George Telek.

Grade 8 dropout is chef & literary prize sponsor
Jeffrey Mane Febi

This is the story of Joe Yagama, 38, whose mother and father are from Sinasina and Bundi respectively. He lives in his mother's village and is happily married with a son who was born recently.

Many a tale of success pops up now and then. This one strikes a chord I am familiar with and to a certain extent I feel I should claim it. Anyway, here's the story.

In 1991, while still in Grade 8, Joe dropped out of Kundiawa's Catholic run Kondiu Rosary High School. Like many young and vulnerable people in the harsh world outside of school, he roamed the streets until 2005, when he got a job as a kitchen hand at the Airways Hotel in Port Moresby.

After nine months and numerous secret lessons from other kitchen staff, he managed to grace his boss's radar and was promoted to trainee pizza chef.

His success at Airways enabled him in 2008 to apply for and secure a new job at the Shady Rest Hotel in Moresby. But after only a few months he found himself on the streets again – thanks to workplace lies, deceit and jealousy.

But fate wasn't finished with Joe yet. In 2009 he was working for minerals explorer Marengo Gold at its Yandera exploration camps in Bundi. This experience in the extractive industry was to prove crucial.

He applied for and was offered a position with Kutubu Catering Limited – the company that feeds the entire Oil Search Limited (OSL) operations in the Kutubu and surrounding project areas. He was posted to OSL's drilling rig 103 where I'm stationed and the rest is history.

Currently he is night chef – a position that requires him to manage the Rig 103 camp at night apart from his kitchen duties. He has handled things well despite the camp's mix of international inhabitants and their demands for peculiar dishes.

What interests me about Joe is his recent revelation during a casual chat. He is sponsoring a literature competition at Giu Primary School this school year.

I, upon hearing about his project, at once lit up and pestered him to tell me more.

The school is located in Dinga No 2 in the Suai LLG area of Sina Sina-Yongomugl district of Simbu Province.

Joe stated that through the competition he aims to "motivate and spark passion in students from this rural school to focus on achieving and aim high".

What really intrigues me is the question of why would Joe, given his education background, sponsor a competition that could potentially alleviate the level of spoken and written English in this part of Simbu, let alone the other positive effects it may generally have over students from Giu?

It appears Joe is an educated and intelligent man, albeit without formal qualifications. He is aware of the positive impact the English language can have on students of Giu Primary School and is actually doing something to enable students to learn to write and speak in English better.

Like Joe there are thousands of Grade 8 dropouts in villages, towns and cities across the country. Grade 10 and 12 dropouts are also plentiful. If all can think and do something to help themselves and their respective communities without doubt there wouldn't be anyone left to cultivate and nurture the cargo cult mentality.

If only we all could do our bit, however little it may be for the country, we will all be meaningful participants in the development of this country and may turn this country around from its path to self- destruction overnight – if overnight is too fast than in matter of a decade.

I am referring to people-driven change and not government driven change as many a time changes or proposed changes sponsored by the government is always hijacked by a member of, to use Martyn Namorong's words, the predatory elite class.

I think Joe is doing something noble and have contemplated supporting him in his endeavour. He is aware of and has tried to view and read *PNG Attitude* but poor network reception at our workplace has denied him access.

I had a dream last night: A vision for my country
Danny Gonnol

I was my mother's only child when Papua New Guinea became an independent nation. The PNG flag was raised for the first time and the Australian flag was lowered for the last time. That was 16 September 1975.

As the years passed, I enrolled to commence my primary education. That was in the 1980s at the Alkena Lutheran Primary School.

Every morning we would assemble, sing the national anthem, raise the flag and shout the national pledge.

"We the people of PNG pledge ourselves, united in one nation, we pledge to build a democratic society based on justice, equality, respect and prosperity for our people, and we pledge to stand together as one people, one nation, and one country."

I did not understand why we had to do that.

In class, I was taught by my teachers about a country called Papua New Guinea. I learnt about its history, geography, politics and government. I was taught that a man called Michael Somare fought for and gained independence.

As my young brain developed, all these became fascinating stories. They were comparable to fairy tales and the mythical legends my mother would tell me in the dark of night.

That was not the end. My love to explore landed me at a place at Tambul High School. It was about this time that my knowledge of PNG grew. At high school, I came in contact with students from the various tribes of the Western Highlands.

The 1990s were the beginning of a new dawn in my life. The strings of attachment were loosened as I flew out of the Western Highlands to a land my ancestors knew not. It was there that I became nationally conscious. That was at Sogeri National High School.

I met students from all parts of our country. I realised I was no longer confined to my cage of tribalism, provincialism or regionalism. Rather, I belonged to a national family, a vibrant independent nation called Papua New Guinea.

The year 1991 was a memorable year. It was the year the 9th South Pacific Games was staged in Port Moresby. Tears of joy literally ran down my cheeks as my country men and women ran to victory not with ordinary medals but gold medals.

For the first time I could see fellow Papua New Guineans united in one mind freely expressing the spirit of national unity and pride. The support for our participants was overwhelming. Patriotic spectators were waving the golden coloured PNG flag to signal victory at hand.

My love and attachment for this country was given a positive boost when I enrolled for legal studies at the University of Papua New Guinea in the 1990s. Here I met a number of young like-minded Papua New Guineans of my age who shared the same views as I.

We discussed in our daily conversations nothing but issues concerning our country. It was also about this time that the Barike Hit song *One Country, One People, One Nation* was released. It broke everyone's heart including mine.

Whilst at university I was accorded the opportunity to travel overseas. My trip took me to Australia. This trip changed my views of my country. At Sydney's international airport I saw huge planes. In the midst I saw a small plane. It carried the flag of our country. It was a plane operated by Air Niugini. Within me flowed a feeling of smallness. As I imagined how small is our country, tears of patriotism flowed freely.

The same trip took me to Melbourne. I missed the train watching a street man dressed in Scottish attire playing bagpipes. My other colleagues left me. I was lost in that city in the late hours of the afternoon.

Being there for the first time, I did not know where to go, losing all sense of direction and contact with the hotel room we were staying. I planned to sleep on the streets if I could not make it back to the hotel.

From a distance, I heard someone shouting *"wantok"*. I looked across, the face looked familiar. It was the face of a Tolai. As my eyes met his, red hot tears started falling. We hugged, cried and cried. We did not care we were in another country.

He asked if I could go with him in order that his family meet me. His kids needed to see a PNG uncle. I accepted his invitation. When we arrived at his home, his family gave me a reception I never expected. Though I was a stranger, I was treated more than a brother. I felt at home.

The family played a collection of PNG music including the national anthem. I never felt the feeling of attachment to this country more so than that night with a Tolai family in Melbourne.

A small PNG flag, hanging on the wall meant more than just a *laplap* printed in PNG colours. One will go overseas to experience what I experienced. If there was anything I gained from that trip, it elevated me to become a national patriot and a nationalist in its true sense.

I realise, this is the kind of feeling that must have led President John F Kennedy to declare *"Ask not what your country can do for you but ask what you can do for your country."*

When I returned I felt more Papua New Guinean. To me every person across this nation is my brother under one flag from the far eastern end of Bougainville to the northern tip of Manus, to the border provinces of Western and Sandaun to the far southern ends of Milne Bay.

I don't care whether you are from the Highlands or Momase, New Guinea Highlands or the Southern regions, you are my countryman. I am proud of you. Together we shall move this nation forward.

Like Martin Luther King I have a dream. It is a national dream. It is a Papua New Guinean Dream.

One day, someday, PNG shall rise. It shall rise to become the focus of world attention. Nations of the earth shall shout. *"This is the land."* It is but only a dream.

I have nothing but a dream. One day, someday, law and order will be restored in this land. Men of all ages will take drugs and beer no more. Women old and young shall freely walk the streets of Port Moresby, Lae and Mt Hagen.

The effects will be felt in all hamlets, from the misty mountains to the stormy seas and from village communities to urban settlements, until it reaches every corner of this nation. It is but a dream.

I have nothing but a dream. Mothers shall cry no more. Tribal fights shall cease forever. Attitudes of men shall change. Enemies shall walk hand in hand in a brotherly fashion. Justice will be restored, equality observed and corruption no more. It is but a dream.

I have nothing but a dream. A day is coming when man shall not be judged by his wealth, but by his reputation, character and integrity. It is coming when the poor shall say, "I am rich" and the rich shall say, "I am poor." It is but a dream.

I have nothing but a dream. I dream of that day when the volcanic ashes of Rabaul shall settle. The dying frangipani shall bloom. From the blooming flowers shall come forth sweet fragrance.

A fragrance that will cover the island of Manus and overflow to the border town of Vanimo and all the way to the gold fields of Porgera, the gas fields of Hela and the tea fields of Jiwaka. The effects will be felt in the maritime provinces of Milne Bay, Oro, and Western. It is but a dream.

I have nothing but a dream. A wind of change is blowing. It is blowing from the peaks of Mt. Giluwe. It is sweeping across the nation from the mighty plains of the Waghi Valley, to the muddy waters of the Sepik.

More than that, it is moving from the Owen Stanley Ranges, penetrating the Rockies of Simbu to the oily waters of the Gulf and to the grasslands of Central. It is shaking the foundations of this nation. It is felt in the troubled island of Bougainville, the mighty Markham valley and the far corners of Enga. It is but a dream.

Chains are breaking. Change is coming. Light is emerging. Darkness no more. Goroka jumps in surprise. Kimbe bows in silence. Wewak stands at ease. Popondetta rises in confusion. Kavieng watches in amazement. Madang salutes. Mendi celebrates. PNG rises to world attention. It is but a dream.

I have nothing but a dream. I dream of that day when every boy, girl, man and woman shall joyfully proclaim: *"Port Moresby is my political Capital, Lae is my industrial capital, Mt Hagen is my financial capital and PNG is my country."* It is but a dream.

When that day comes, the nations of the world shall flock to this land of old and share in its blessings. They shall know why God the Creator gave a thousand tongues, a thousand nations within a nation - *Papua New Guinea unity in diversity*. At last my dream last night stands fulfilled.

The people of Western Highlands spoke: *"Your time has not come."* They did not give me the mandate to govern. I did not win, but the principles I stood for were not defeated. I am down but not out. Some fine day the principles I stood for will rise. They will rise like an eagle in flight.

Stability for whom? – The ambiguity of our future
Gary Juffa

One of the current questions doing the rounds in Papua New Guinea is whether centralisation of power will ensure political stability and, if so, will stability translate to tangible development for the ordinary Papua New Guineans?

This question stems from the PNG government's efforts to ensure political stability through proposed amendments to the Constitution - specifically Section 145 which makes a destabilising vote of no confidence provision available to PNG's parliamentarians.

The provision allows a vote of no confidence to be brought about by disgruntled members if they can muster 10% of parliamentarians and move a motion on the floor with almost no notice.

This provision has ensured that, since Papua New Guinea's independence, there has never been a political party remain in power long enough to bring about tangible development. At least that's the excuse used by those who have been ousted via that process.

Then a new law on the Integrity of Political Parties stopped members from hopping to and from political parties whenever they felt like it, usually motivated by self-interest and ego. Later the provisions of that law were removed to allow members to do as they please and hop about again.

This brought PNG back to the dreaded vote of no confidence. The National Alliance government was immediately thrown out after almost 10 years of so-called stability. Nothing of any real positive significance was achieved during this period.

Corporations, especially in fisheries, logging and mining, flourished. They paid little tax, were given many exemptions and made great profits.

Several companies in the forestry sector shifted from raping forests to building supermarkets and exploring new business ventures, whilst still paying minimal tax.

Many of these businesses were built on government land pilfered or otherwise acquired through suspicious means. A piece of land at Waigani was somehow obtained by a Lands Board Member and "sold" for a hefty profit to one such firm.

Such stories are so numerous that, even though outrageous, they are no longer spoken of, just accepted and expected.

So is this recent effort to centralise power going to guarantee the stability the government claims it will?

We would all like to believe. But there are many people who do not; the Opposition for instance plans to take the matter to court.

Professor John Nonggorr, a reputable Papua New Guinean lawyer, does not believe so either and has stated that the effort is not in the interests of the people.

And a recent online comment from the Economist Intelligence Unit referred to it as "undemocratic". The EIU did, however, forecast a stable political environment for the period 2012 to 2017. That is a foreign economic perspective.

What I would like to know is what does political stability really mean for ordinary Papua New Guineans? Does it translate to economic progress that they want and need?

I am particularly concerned about the thieves and liars who mill around the spheres of power, concocting scams and schemes to siphon off public funds and deliver half-baked projects. Will they be held accountable for what they have done?

Will they be prevented from their stealing, lying and misuse? Will anyone be prosecuted? Will there ever be justice for the people? Will, for instance, the K500 million misused and basically stolen in the 2008–12 National Agriculture Development Program scam ever be recovered or the perpetrators brought to justice?

And what about the K230 millions of RESI (Rehabilitation of Education Sector Infrastructure) funds in that same period? This year K500 million for tertiary institutions was earmarked to be managed by the Ministry for Higher Education.

(Incidentally the Minister was earlier this year urging the handing over of K5 million in road funding to a subsidiary of a logging firm.)

Another question I pose here is whether political stability has ever delivered justice?

One must reflect on numerous instances of misuse of public funds over the years perpetrated by elected leaders and their minions. There have been many examples of this since 16 September 1975 and a trend has developed: no one is ever taken to task; no one is ever prosecuted; no property or resources that belonged to the people have been recovered. Ever.

It seems that in PNG, crime of this magnitude pays. To this day, this trend does not seem to be changing for the better.

Numerous inquiries have led nowhere, no one has been charged or prosecuted, scams within scams, and enormous amount of public monies wasted.

The examples are many, but I will just mention a recent inquiry. The SABL Inquiry cost K15 million that could have purchased 60 double classrooms, 150 ambulances, a small hospital and enough medication to save lives, or maybe a decent road or bridge somewhere making access to health, education and justice possible for people in remote areas.

Of course, these estimates do not factor in the middle men fees and bogus feasibility studies and so forth inevitably associated with the delivery of anything via the public service.

The SABL Inquiry is just another example of issues that remain "unresolved" - swept under the carpet and in time forgotten. Eventually future generations will have no inkling that such a substantial amount of money was thrown into a giant black hole. There are many more examples: the Finance Inquiry, Sandline Inquiry, Motigate, Cairns Conservatory, National Provident Fund and so forth.

So how can political stability translate to development if nothing is ever done to take out the garbage?

Let me rephrase: If no one is unable to stand up and take to task those who have stolen substantial public monies and put in place effective controls to prevent the fraud and theft that is so rampant now what use is political stability?

Certainly the corporate world welcomes political stability because it allows companies to plan confidently and invest with some foresight. They can manage the costs of running their businesses with little concern for unforeseen costs associated with an unstable political environment.

They can forecast their profits and expenses and obtain loans with more ease. Banks and other financial institutions like politically stable economies. They're great for business!

But if this does not translate to tangible development for the people then how useful is it? Development should not only mean an improvement in general living standards but also the delivery of justice, in this case, the punishment of those involved in stealing or squandering public monies.

While efforts are being made to provide so-called political stability in Papua New Guinea, aggressive land grabbing and illegal exploitation of the people's resources continues unabated.

Just travel anywhere in PNG and spend some time in the villages and towns. Look at the logging camps of the Gulf and Western provinces where resource owners are recruited as ill-paid labour to harvest their own timber.

They have the privilege of earning some coins which are promptly spent at the tucker boxes or mini-marts in these same logging camps. It's akin to modern day slavery.

Look at the hordes of illegal fishing vessels that anchor off the waters of PNG waiting for the cover of darkness to enter in search of shark fin - cutting off fins for this lucrative but heinous trade and sending the sharks back into the ocean to slowly die a horrible death.

Look at the predators that enter Western Province to hunt for crocodiles, deer, Saratoga and barramundi - shooting indiscriminately at villagers who wander by. These villagers have become too frightened to venture into their own forests to hunt or farm.

Meanwhile, the government is still entertaining Nautilus Ltd and its Solwara 1 seabed mining project that seeks to pioneer another destructive effort in the seas of PNG despite the law and despite the objections of more than 20,000 Papua New Guineans.

Our leaders who not so long ago insisted they were concerned about their people have done an about faces and suddenly promote the Nautilus project proclaiming "pioneering revolutionary technology" and espousing the great economic boom that can come about from such projects.

What they fail to say is that the great economic boom is not for the people who have lived there for hundreds of years or more and call it their home. Apparently they do not matter - at least not until the 2017 election.

Then the usual suspects hoping for election or re-election will expound their usual rhetoric of declaring great things for the people and the country and denouncing corruption.

Now let's add to these concerns the issue of the fugitive Djoko Tjandra, wanted by Interpol and Indonesia for massive bank fraud. Tjandra managed to enter Papua New Guinea in July last year just a day before he was to front up in the Jakarata Supreme Court.

In Port Moresby he was met and greeted by the then Minister for Foreign Affairs (with 10 boxes of blue label Johnny Walker), granted PNG citizenship in record time and issued a PNG passport despite the fact that PNG is a signatory to the United Nations Convention of Transnational Crimes which stipulates that signatories cooperate in the investigation and prosecution of such criminals.

To add salt to the wound, a company Tjandra is associated with, Naima Rice Project Ltd, has been given the green light to proceed with plans to monopolise the commercialisation of rice in Papua New Guinean – and was even granted funds by the Department of Agriculture to conduct research and prepare a submission.

This is of course not the end of it. It is now revealed that Tjandra's relatives who already have citizenship are embarking on a venture that will see them control the *buai* industry. This same group of people killed the vanilla industry in PNG by monopolising the purchase of vanilla and encouraging improper processing that saw international markets close their doors on what could have been a potential money maker for the ordinary people of PNG.

There is even more. Perhaps one wants to contemplate the efforts being made to re-open the Panguna mine. Again, the people who matter are not being considered and leaders are enthusiastically signing paper and making grandiose speeches without considering the reasons why the mine led to a civil war that lasted 10 years, destroyed an island and cost 20,000 lives with many more people affected to this very day.

Or maybe we can discuss what benefits Porgera and

other such mines have really brought to the local people in those areas. Sure we got much revenue but where did that revenue go?

Many people will no doubt defend the mining industry, but I would like Papua New Guineans to think whether their districts and stations and towns are better off. They are not. They are rotting. Filled with decaying colonial era infrastructure and unfinished overpriced and dubiously paid projects that were either scams from the beginning or, in some rare cases, great ideas hijacked by the self-interested.

There is no shortage of stories told about the exploitation of the people's land, timber, marine resources and much else. There is also no shortage of stories of neglect of the people by the very governments elected time and time again promising wealth, development and a better life but instead delivering failed projects, scams and schemes.

No matter what people say, and there are those who profusely defend the government, one can carry out a simple test to determine the validity of my claim.

Take a drive to any District station, let's say Kwikila, or Kupiano, maybe Kokoda, or how about Banz. Or Tapini. Select any District in any Province and take a trip there.

Your own observation and research will satisfy you that there has been no progress.

Easier still, take a stroll through any government department and observe what happens there. Take note of the level of dress and professionalism, punctuality, cleanliness, written and spoken speech, and assess the credibility of some of our senior public servants and ask how they got there and consider whether they would ever be employed in a corporate entity anywhere.

So what guarantee is there that stability will ensure development? What guarantee is there that stability will ensure that the thieves and plunderers still in the parliament will give up scheming and concocting ideas of how to steal the people's money. Will they ever be stopped or brought to justice? Ever?

There is really no guarantee that political stability will bring true development. If true development can be brought about without justice, then I am wrong.

Until then, I await the promised reshuffle. Will some of the garbage be taken out? If so, I am hopeful that political stability in this instance may work. If not, then let's brace ourselves for another round of scams, schemes, lies, theft and general misconduct by our so-called leaders.

Perhaps the people will come to their senses in 2017, mobilise and nominate their own champions and elect them – regardless of existing political parties, campaign rhetoric and seasoned party strategies promoted every five years.

Or maybe PNG will continue down the slippery slope of anarchy, chaos, illegal land grabbing, marginalisation of land owners, destruction of forests and oceans, disease and rampant crime and corruption until we are in such a mess as to satisfy foreign powers to enter on the pretext of saving us from ourselves and our inability to govern our future.

Who knows really.

Fijians: Melanesians like PNGns but a class above
David Kitchnoge

This is an article I wrote way back in 2006 at the waiting lounge at Nadi international airport when I visited Fiji for the first time on a business trip. I shared it with my circle of friends when I returned to PNG. Now I would like to make it available to a wider audience

Fellow Papua New Guineans I've just returned from a short trip to Fiji and what an eye-opener it was. Fijians are Melanesians like us but they definitely are a class above. They are a nation of well groomed, calm and very organised individuals. I couldn't help but envy the free night life of the Fijian capital of Suva where you can walk down the streets without the concern of being attacked or harassed by thugs.

There is a barbecue going on at major sections of the streets in Suva and both residents and visitors alike can go along and enjoy themselves with their families.

There are countless numbers of top-notch restaurants where you can go and be served really nice meals at an affordable price.

Ladies, and I mean females, girls, walk around the streets freely in the night and no one touches them. This would have to rank among the top five luxuries for our women in PNG but, that's 'life as usual' for Fijians. And their streets are much cleaner and pleasant than ours.

Their population is almost evenly split between the indigenous Fijians and the Indo-Fijians but just about everyone is very friendly and easy to get along with. Everywhere you go, you are greeted with wide smiles accompanied by a *bula* (welcome/greeting). And every public announcement made over the inter-com ends with a *vinaka* (thank you) or the longer version *vinaka vakalevu* (thank you very much).

No one told me but it is probably an unwritten fact that the Fijians are acutely aware of the importance of tourism on their economy and ultimately their well-being, hence the appropriate behaviour.

Fiji doesn't have the kind of mines (gold, copper, nickel etc) that we have plus our rich marine resources and forestry but they are richer than us in terms of GDP per capita and the real life on the ground.

All they have are sugar cane, fisheries, and mostly tourism unlike us who appear to be endowed with endless amounts of resources. This is truly one of the greatest paradoxes in our region.

So what does that tell us about the Fijians and us? I think one explanation for that would be in this word – efficiency.

Fijians are very efficient operators and gain the maximum benefit out of their scarce resources whilst we, on the other hand, are a very inefficient nation who wastes all our resources on non-productive and non-value adding activities. We are truly a nation that is so rich yet so poor.

Apart from that, I think one of the biggest differences between us and them as a people is that we have very different temperaments. They appeared to me to be a calm, peaceful, gentle, respectful and tolerant people while we are the exact opposite.

We are a country of bigheads, arrogant and violent people who will not hesitate to prey on someone's misfortune. No wonder tourism will never be a sustainable industry in our beautiful country.

The reasons why we are worse off than them or they are better off than us (whichever way you see it) can be many and varied but one thing is for sure. The biggest gulf between our fellow Melanesian brothers and sisters and us is attitude.

We can match and even better them when and only when we change our bad attitudes. I pray that this happens in my lifetime.

Down the Fly River, this time with a paddle
Martyn Awayang Namorong

On Tuesday I arrived in Port Moresby after a six month stint at the Ok Tedi copper-gold mine in the Star Mountains of western Papua New Guinea.

The experience was overwhelmingly positive and gave me many insights into the political economy of the resources sector in PNG and Western Province in particular.

Towards the end of last year, I observed and participated in discussions that led to 156 communities signing up to extend the mine life at Ok Tedi beyond 2015.

What stunned me about the discussions was the amount of scientific information given to the village leaders. It was as if Ok Tedi Mining Limited (OTML) had put itself on trial and gave the leaders evidence against itself.

I do not believe the discussions would have had a positive outcome had it not been for such level of transparency and openness.

So why was the decision to extend the life of the mine a positive outcome?

Firstly, much of the damage has already been done to the Ok Tedi and Fly Rivers. Even if the mine were to close today, the riverine impacts from BHP operations will be around for 200 years.

Mine life extension will have a net benefit for the Ok Mani, Ok Tedi and Fly rivers in that OTML will continue to add limestone to for another 10 years, improving the acid-base balance of the river systems.

In addition the dredging of the Ok Tedi River at Bige will continue at current levels during mine life extension, even though Ok Tedi will be operating a smaller mine at 60% of current mining operations.

Communities down river also have the opportunity to enjoy a further 10 years of economic and social benefits from the mine as a result of what's termed the Community Mine Continuation Extension Agreement (CMCAEA).

I didn't meet anyone at Tabubil who denied Ok Tedi's devastating environmental legacy. I did meet many people who were keen to do the right thing by the people and the environment.

In these circumstances, it has been quite distressing for me to see the recent turn of events regarding Ok Tedi.

As my contract with OTML has expired and I no longer work for the company, I feel compelled to tell the truth about Ok Tedi.

Readers may recall a *Post Courier* article and several blog posts about women on the Fly River dying of a mysterious bleeding illness. Opportunists took advantage of these stories to accuse Ok Tedi of causing this dreadful outcome.

It took independent journalist Jo Chandler to find that the cause of the bleeding was cervical cancer.

Chandler wrote regarding the 'mysterious' bleedings:

PNG has among the highest rates of cervical cancer in the world; the disease kills at least 700 women a year. Kebei's imminent death, at 49 years of age, may be unfathomable in the Australian context.

But without early detection (pap smear screening), treatment (PNG has a single overworked radiotherapy machine, and access to chemotherapy and surgery is extremely limited) and prevention (HPV vaccine, while it holds great promise for developing nations, remains financially beyond reach), in PNG her death is no mystery.

Cervical cancer is caused by the human papilloma virus (HPV) and has nothing to do with waste from the Ok Tedi mine.

Since 2002, OTML has paid K10 billion in taxes and dividends to the PNG government. Yet during the debate that ensued regarding the poor health of Fly River women, no one (including the blogs and newspapers) asked the government how it had used all that money for the benefit of those women or to improve oncology services.

So why have all these parties with vested interest been attacking Ok Tedi Mining Limited, the Ok Tedi Development Foundation(OTDF) and the PNG Sustainable Development Program (PNGSDP)?

I won't answer that question but if you are a journalist or blogger wanting to know the truth, go to the Waigani Courthouse on 8 April.

There, an interesting court case will be heard regarding K69 million from the Western Province People's Dividend Trust Fund - a fund that holds dividends from Ok Tedi.

There you will find that some people are wolves in sheep's clothing.

Should OTDF, OTML and PNGSDP be doing more for the people of the Fly River? I believe these organisations can, as they have the resources and capacity to do a lot of good.

I believe the Governor of Western Province, Ati Wobiro recognises this as well and that he will work with them to improve development indicators in the province.

As a Western Province man, I see great potential in such cooperation.

The reality on the ground in Western Province is that OTDF, OTML and PNGSDP are the main parties working to improve conditions.

While others just puff hot air in Waigani or in cyberspace, these organisations are travelling down the Fly River with a paddle.

PNG development: We need a coup in the chicken coop
Martyn Awayang Namorong

One dark evening I was plotting revolution with comrade Nou Vada when he brought up this interesting scenario of the chickens in the coop.

No chickens were harmed in the creation of this metaphor but comrade Nou described a profound condition of the Papua New Guinean psyche - at least amongst chooks.

Basically Nou, or whoever he got the idea from, describes some people as being like chickens that have been kept in a coop for too long.

The chickens are so used to receiving chicken feed so that once you throw the key into the cage, the chickens throw the key back to you and ask for more feed

So I'm adding chicken to the already well known sheeple.

I witnessed these chicken exchanges recently as community leaders here in the Western Province discussed regional development.

Following the presentation of a major development organisation about empowering villagers to make decisions regarding their development needs, one of the leaders got agitated and spoke.

I'm paraphrasing what the village leader said but it went along the lines of: "You (donor) know what our problems are, just deliver on our development needs."

Anyway the donor representative replied diplomatically that the villagers should submit their development needs to have them assessed instead of the donor deciding what the people needed.

In much of the discourse about development, there is talk about empowering communities and ensuring the self-sustainability of aid projects.

But what happens when you give communities the opportunities for progress and they fail to make use of them to create better outcomes?

As difficult as it may be for some people to accept, there is a role for so-called handouts.

If the chickens in the coop won't use the key to set themselves free, you have to continue with the chicken feed or else they'll starve to death.

Papua New Guineans love to bash major donors and their boomerang aid, but we need to reflect as to whether we use the keys they sometimes throw into the coop to set ourselves free.

Before a revolution can take place in the communities, we need a coup in the coop.

Road to hell is paved with religion & westernisation
Martyn Awayang Namorong

When the greedy white ruling class decided to loot the rest of the world's nations of their wealth they carried with them, their laws, their customs, their government, their technology, their diseases and their religion.

The greatest lessons about how the west and by extension the western model of development work can be found in the way they shamelessly conducted themselves in other peoples land.

Their religion Christianity was about a Middle-Eastern zombie. (FYI a zombie is something that rises from the dead). They told everyone that their religion was the only way to spiritual heaven.

The historical context of colonization is that it was coming out of a people who had for millennia since the Greek empire of Alexander, being a subversive race. First the Greeks, followed by the Romans, then the Roman Catholic Church and the European nations. They had thousands of years of experience in subverting people.

At the time Europeans decided to subvert nations elsewhere, their Religion was is turmoil thanks to a German Priest (my namesake a German Priest called Martin) who noted that the religious center of the Western model of Development, was rotten to the core.

The Catholic priests had, after centuries of wanking in monasteries, figured how to subvert people in order to exploit them off their wealth.

I'm deliberately using the word 'subversion' or 'subvert' because to subvert a population is to make the population think that it is acting in its best Interest while at the same time undermining its interest. In simple English: they make you think you're helping yourself when in fact you're harming yourself.

In order to build St Peter's Basilica in Rome they made the Europeans think that it was in their interest to give money to the Catholic Church for the remission of sins - some con job the poppies called indulgence. The premise of this was that Jesus is the only way to Spiritual heaven and the Western Church is the only way to a Middle-Eastern zombie.

So the Church thrived at the expense of the poor Europeans and the Europeans genuinely thought they were serving their best interest, until my namesake (Martin) figured the con job. Having being challenged by Martin Luther, the Church launched the Counter-Reformation. The word propaganda was first used when Pope Gregory XIII (1572-85) set up the Societas de Propaganda Fide (Society for the Propagation of Faith).

This narrative continues today not just in the one way to spiritual heaven version, but also the one way to physical heaven version. The contest for the monopoly of religious and secular ways into heaven have continued down the centuries including during the Cold War. Indeed the Cold War is a classic contest of ideas, both religious and secular.

We also see today the contest of ideas between the Islamic world and the West. For the West, there can be no other form of government than democracy. Even though, the people of Islamic Iran have higher levels of literacy and education compared to 'democratic' PNG and communist Cuba has better Healthcare than democratic America.

Now, I'm not implying that PNG becomes an Islamic Republic or a Commie state, instead I'm highlighting the fact that different cultures, societies, geographical locations and historical contexts need their own unique sets of ideas to progress.

Today, many people religiously preach that the only way to physical heaven is the western colonial model of development. When my namesake questioned the One Church to Heaven narrative, he was excommunicated, ridiculed and threatened.

It wasn't because he was theologically wrong, it was because some of the Elite in Europe did not wish to give up their control of religion, political power, land and resources.

The western elite set out to conquer the world with their one model of development that would replicate the St Peters Basilica social experiment throughout the world. Papua New Guineans are being hoodwinked today into paying a lot of indulgences (resources exploited by foreigners) in order to get to heaven (see development).

My namesake saw the deceit of the Western Model of Spirituality and argued that it wasn't the Pope (head of the Church and the European elite) who would take people to spiritual heaven; it was the faith of the individual. You didn't have to give your resources to the Pope in order to get to heaven.

It is not necessary that we handover our resources to foreigners in order to see progress. If it was, the founders of these nations would not have called for National Sovereignty and Self Reliance or for the wise use of natural resources or even for our own model of development as articulated by Goal number 5 of the Papua New Guinea Constitution.

Subversion is seen as the ultimate weapon of War. It is also referred to as Political Warfare or diplomacy. It was first described by an ancient Chinese General, Sun Tzu in The Art of War. Sun Tzu writes:

"The Supreme Art of War is to subdue the enemy [a nation] without fighting."

In case you still haven't noticed yet, Papua New Guinea has already been conquered. Different parties have used arguments from the Western Model of Development, to invade the country.

We have a Malaysian who has conquered Logging and Oil Palm

We have the Chinese who have conquered the Retail sector

We have the Americans who have conquered Natural Gas

We have the Commonwealth (Australian/Canadian) miners who have conquered Mining.

We have the Filipinos who have conquered Tuna Fisheries to supply Europeans

I know there are many Papua New Guineans out there dreaming of being rich. But ask yourself, how will you gain wealth if foreigners are in charge of the sources of wealth? How will you develop your country if you don't have control of the resources necessary for creating developmental activities.

The consequence of foreigners being in control of national wealth is that we fight like dogs over elections and positions in politics and the public services, so that we might be able to collect the scraps they throw to the government coffers.

Em bai yu toktok long maus tasol long bringim divelopment, na nogat senis bai kamap. Yu ken tok yu papa na mama graun o yu risos owna tasol samtin tru em yu papa/mama long nem tasol na ol ausait lain benefit.

The West's model of development is a form of violence: Economic Violence. Look no further than Panguna, the Fly River, the Watut River, RH logging Camps, Ramu Mine, SABLs, etc... The reason you don't perceive it as violence is because you've been trained to think that it's ok - just collateral damage [remember subversion].

But just in case you don't believe me look at what's happened to Europes PIGS [PIGS stands for Portugal Ireland Greece & Spain]. Having fattened the PIGS with cheap credit, the Bankers have now taken them to the Economic slaughterhouse to trim the fat.

Germany (Formerly the Holy Roman Empire, and Colonizers of New Guinea) is punishing its neighbors. Previously they fought with armies, now they use Economic Violence. Now they're telling the PIGS that it's perfectly normal and in their interest to suffer economic violence.

Gandhi described poverty as the worst form of violence. But poverty is just a symptom of economic disparity also referred to as economic violence. And economic violence is a product of the greed of a few elite.

And the elite have used the Western Model of Development to enrich themselves the same way that the Catholic Church enriched its coffers with indulgences. They both promise heaven but fail to deliver.

Now you have been trained not to question these two realities: religion and development. No one wants to be anti-god or anti-westernization. If you do stray away from these two sets of belief systems either god will punish you or Americans will bomb your country.

Sun Tzu warns in the Art of War: "Know your enemy and know yourself..."

If Dekla says Papua New Guinea is Eden, then it is!
Francis Sina Nii

In need of Vitamin D from heaven's abundant supply, I was wheeled in my battered wheelchair down to the helipad at the southern end of Kundiawa's Sir Joseph Nombri Memorial hospital, which is my home.

As I was sun bathing, Kaupa, an old friend and an aspiring politician, walked up to me. He had seen me through the window of the ward where his sick daughter had been admitted the day before.

We chatted for a while and Kaupa suggested we go to the hospital front-gate market for a cup of Kongo coffee. He helped me push my wheelchair and we went to the favourite coffee spot.

After a *kapa* each at Dorothy's Coffee Shop, I was tempted to take a chew of betel nut. We moved to the first seller on the Wara Simbu side of the road and I paid for two nuts.

As we were chewing, a young woman in her early thirties came towards us wearing six-pocket trousers, collared tee-shirt and a pair of strappers.

"Dekla, my sister, what are you doing here?" the *buai* seller asked the woman in *Tok Pisin*.

"My sister Paula, it's been a long time," Dekla responded and they shook hands.

"I've been in the hospital for some days now looking after my son. He twisted his ankle while playing with other children and got admitted", Dekla explained.

After chatting with Paula for a while, Dekla asked her for some betel nut. "*Sista sampela piksa buai o* - sister any display nuts?"

"*Sista laip em had tru* - sister life is so difficult. *Buai em ino planti* - betel nuts are not plenty. *Yu baim na kaikai* - you buy and chew," the buai seller responded.

"*Sista, mi askim long wanpela piksa buai tasol* - sister, I am asking for a display nut only. *Blong wanem yu tok laip i had* - why are you saying life is so difficult? *Olsem wanem laip i had tru* – how comes life is so difficult?"

"*Sori sista, laip long town i had tru* – sorry sister, life in town is so hard. *Olgeta samting i moni tasol* - everything is money".

"*Oh sista, yu nogat wok na yu hangamap nating long town olsem na yu painim laip em had* – oh sister, yu have no jobs and you are just squatting in town that's why you find life so difficult. *Yu mas kam bek long ples* – you must come back to the village.

"*Ples em heven* – village is heaven. *Olgeta samting i stap* – everything is in the village. *Yu ino bai wari long wanpela samting* – you will never be worried about anything".

The conversation turned into an argument and became quite bitter so I decided to distract them. I gave K2 to Paula and instructed her to give Dekla four nuts worth 50 toea each.

Dekla looked at me and shook her head. "Give his money back," she said and pulled the K2 from Paula's hand and gave it back to me.

"I feel sorry for you. I have money. I will buy myself some nuts but not from this rubbish," and Dekla pulled out a K10 note out of a roll of ten and twenty kina bills in her purse in full view of Paula and walked to the next seller. Would you like a drink of Coke? She asked me and I nodded.

From the corner of my eyes I saw Paula trying to swallow a lump that refused to go down her throat. I couldn't figure out what was going on in her mind but clearly she was flustered.

Dekla came back with a bottle of Coke and a handful of betel nut and mustard beans. She gave me the Coke and suggested that we stay under the shade of a mango tree on the other side of the road and chew. We went to the shade of the mango tree.

"Paula is my cousin," Dekla explained as she and Kaupa were chewing the nuts and I was drinking the Coke.

"We are from Toromambuno in Gembogl. We both left school after completing grade six and got married.

"Me and my husband, we live in the village. Our three children were born at Gembogl rural health centre.

"Once in a while I travel to Madang or Lae to sell my carrots, broccoli and cauliflowers. After selling them, I buy clothes and household items - mattresses, blankets, cooking pots - that we need and I go back.

"Paula and her husband left the village soon after they got married and they have been living in a settlement around here ever since.

"I don't understand this talk of hard life or poverty. Maybe this is the language of vagrants squatting in settlements in towns and cities.

"In the village, we have everything we need. We have food, fresh clean water, firewood and a house to live in.

"When we are hungry, we just take a walk to the back of our house and pick ripe bananas, avocado or sugar cane and consume them and we are full.

"When we need salt, soap, kerosene, cooking oil or a FlexCard to make a phone call, we pick coffee or vegetables from the garden and sell them on the roadside, get the money and we buy these things.

"We are not worried about money. We don't struggle in the scorching heat to make a few kinas for just one evening's meal.

"We do gardening whenever we feel like. Otherwise we go washing in the creek or lazing around with friends and play 7 Bomb - cards. We are happy.

"I feel sorry for my sister and her family. They must come back to the village," Dekla said.

I was very interested in what Dekla said especially after all the negative publicity about PNG in the Australian media following the asylum seeker deal. I mulled over her words for a while and then asked her a question.

"Dekla, contrary to what you have said, some Australians are saying that PNG is a poverty stricken shithole. What do you think about that?" I stressed every word for effect.

"What?" Kaupa and Dekla fumed simultaneously.

"Lucky their jobless are living off the dole otherwise they would starve to death". So said Kaupa, the senior public servant and aspiring politician.

"People like Paula who squat in settlements and lack basic needs like food, good shelter and decent clothes may come under the definition of poverty that Australians are talking about. But that's only a fraction of the whole population. Most Papua New Guineans, including me and my people in Salt Nomane, are not poor.

"We don't survive on dole handouts. We don't live in makeshift tents. We don't survive on a spoonful of donated rice and soup day by day. We don't stand in queues for hours just to get a bucket of water for a week."

Dekla cut in. "You are right my brother. Papua New Guinea is Eden. We don't lack anything, so why should outsiders describe us as poor people?"

I intervened and changed the subject. After all, the nuts were depleted. We dispersed. And I forgot about the incident.

Is sorcery real or just a myth?
Here's our dilemma
Francis Sina Nii

All the hullabaloo and hype on sorcery in recent times has been focused on the sorcery killers.

Almost all sectors of PNG society condemned the sorcery killings. The O'Neill government, riding on the wave of popular public outcry, has now repealed the Sorcery Act and passed new laws that will see sorcery killers facing the harshest penalty, death.

This is fine as far as protecting the innocent is concerned. However, what hangs in limbo is the question of whether sorcery is real or just a myth.

If it is real, and the accused practitioner proven guilty by scientific means, for example DNA tests, can that person be held accountable?

Sorcery and sorcery killings are common throughout Papua New Guinea. People believe in sorcery. It has long been part of PNG's culture and inheritance since prehistory.

Each culture has its own type of sorcery and sorcery practices.

In some cultures, people are using physical media like lime (*kol kambang* mainly in the New Guinea Islands and northern regions), barks or leaves of certain trees and plants, and carvings made of wood or stone (stone man of Pangia and Erave). In other cultures, they use non-physical supernatural spirits, called *sanguma*.

Sanguma (witchcraft) is the most predominant form of sorcery. It is believed to be responsible for most of the sorcery-related deaths that have been reported.

Sanguma is believed to be a person who presents in the form of an animal or insect of supernatural power. The spirit, through its supernatural power, enables the host to perform incredible acts mostly malevolent and harmful to humans.

The host, enabled by the supernatural power of the medium, can kill another human being by removing an organ or a vital body part. Alternatively, the *sanguma* can remotely control a person by causing fatal accidents and other acts.

Let me exemplify the judicial problem by building a hypothetical case.

A man is accused of killing a young woman through *sanguma*. The man is brought before a legally constituted council of witchdoctors in the presence of police, a judge and local authorities.

The council is told that the accused, using *sanguma*, removed the heart of a young woman and kept it in a dish of water and it can't be put back.

To prove that the heart is actually missing, a post mortem is done on the corpse. The heart is missing, which is witnessed by all.

The authorities then ask the council if the heart can be brought before them. The dead heart is brought before the authorities in a dish.

A DNA test is done on the heart and the young woman. The result confirms that the heart belongs to the young woman.

What will happen to the sorcerer murderer? Should he be set free?

State of Origin: The game that sends PNG bananas
Francis Sina Nii

If there is anything Australian that makes Papua New Guinea go mad then it is the State of Origin rugby league game.

While State of Origin is entertainment, fame and money for Australians, here in PNG it is obsession and fanaticism.

No other sporting event has such a fanatical following. The whole nation goes bananas about the tri-series annual contest that pits the Queensland Maroon boys against the Blue boys from the New South Wales.

The Blues and Maroons culture is growing and spreading even into the remotest communities of PNG.

Children as young as one or two years old are indoctrinated into the Blues and Maroons tribes by their parents. Birthday presents are Blues and Maroons souvenirs.

The kids grow up in Blues and Maroons uniforms. They know the players by name. Show a five or six year old urban kid a picture of Hayne or Thurston and he will call the name and the player's jersey number. No mistake.

The days of the series are unofficial national holidays in PNG. Public servants work only half a day. The other half day they go into celebration.

Families go shopping in the name of Blues and Maroons. They go over their budget to buy TV screens just for the sake of watching the State of Origin games.

Favourite Blues and Maroons team flags fly on hats, motor vehicles and homes as early as Tuesday.

Men, women, boys and girls adorned in Blues and Maroons jerseys or tee-shirts fill the streets, their faces painted in team colours. School children leave classes to get their faces painted.

Young men and women in the rural areas risk their lives and travel hundreds of kilometres to urban areas simply to watch the 80-minute football fixture.

In all of its madness, this is the time that family members divide, Christians don't go to night fellowship, workmates become foes, and best friends become enemies - all in the name of the Blues and Maroons.

The fever heats up as the countdown ticks to the last minute.

Anxiety and unease dig deep within the hearts and minds of die-hard supporters as their eyes are glued to the TV in front of them. Fox Media brings the Telstra Cup to PNG live courtesy of EMTV.

The crazy shouts of the opposing fans ring high as their teams run onto the field for the battle of the stature, power, tact and agility.

'Go Blues...go! Go...Mighty Blues...go!', urges the Blues tribe.

What makes you think the NSW Mighty Blues cannot defeat the Queensland Maroons again in the second fixture of this series tomorrow night?

140 character wit and wisdom
Elvina P Ogil

Elvina Ogil is one of a number of prolific, somewhat profane and occasionally profound denizens of Twitter from Papua New Guinea. The following thoughts provide a glimpse into what appears to be a frenetic life, always conducted at warp speed and with an eye to the foolish and the ridiculous. This edited selection spans a typical week.

Mum says reproachfully "You're driving like a highlander!" Well mother, your children are highlanders and Land Cruisers are highlander cars!

Oh please! KRudd support for gay marriage was so contrived!

The DJs on NauFM are sad, depressing and just plain dumb!

90% of the crowd in court in PNG are here for the free air conditioning!

Can we introduce legislation to ban the *gris pik* perm?

Is it "Come to work looking like a hooker" day today? Erry body dressed like a hooker today (except me of course).

All I know is the roads at Waigani need Jesus!

My dear Highlands sisters, don't be rolling out your house with the perm looking extra greasy but not wearing deodorant! Sort that shit out!

Christ, this Essendon AFL story is a whole pile of who-gives-a-damn.

Listening to Hagen parents watching TV *ba you harim "ahhh ka yee!"* Haha!
And I know I'm riiiiiight! For the first time in my life!

One glass of red and I'm tipsy! What has become of me?

Dear PNG men, saying "psst" and then twitching like you have epilepsy is not a way to pick up women. Maybe in an insane asylum. Not here.

My sisters asking me for support during pregnancy tests crack me up. Um, you didn't ask for my support during the ride did you?

The courthouse: where POM's most sartorially challenged females strut their stuff!

It wasn't actually a constitutional crisis. Nothing was/is wrong with the constitution just the people abusing it.

Attempting a slick walk into work gets ruined when your cousins roar past in a ten seater yelling out your village name!

Birthing classes? Seriously what a wank! Aren't women's bodies designed for childbirth?

Some1needs to tap Luke Matthew on the shoulder and say "You were running for an LLG seat, you dimwit, not president of the free world!"

Western Highlanders protesting the electoral commission decision by closing down the "city"? *Plis nogat sem blo yupla!*

The mood in WHP should be one of collective embarrassment at your dysfunction and wanton violence.

Is Paias Wingti on Twitter from his man-cave? Because he needs 2 get out & sort his kanaka people the hell out! This is such bullshit!

Let's not blame democracy. The people of Hagen Central are uncivilised kanakas.

Mandela had an interesting life. Not you fat mamas in the burbs with your 4 feral kids updating every minute!

It is truly vile that people think their suburban lives are interesting.

What is with [Post-Courier] publishing a picture of people "looking for lice" as a w'end activity? WHAT IS WRONG WITH YOU!

Well it is *The Daily Excrement*! :) Yesterday they had a picture and caption on "looking for lice!" Nitwits!

Some mums talk like they invented children.That stuffs been goin on since Adam & Eve. Your kid is not special, well, not that kind of special.

Some of these women with weaves in Pompomcity walking around looking like they're wearing a tiger cub on their heads!

Dear Hitron, advertising for a "general office GIRL" is outdated, sexist and plain wrong. Get your shit together. Its 2013.

She who claims never to had plastic surgery! *Blari flat screen type face ya*!

What is with PNG people taking photos of the dead? It's

macabre and just wrong.

I nearly punched this wanker taking pics of my uncle today....

If you can afford a carton of beer every weekend you can afford a car. Bloody useless relatives expecting me to drive them everywhere!

Chinese businesses pose problems for PNG
Ishmael Palipal

Chinese businesses are flourishing in all parts of Papua New Guinea and are gradually encroaching upon Bougainville.

The Chinese population and their businesses are increasing. Many Chinese are illegal immigrants and, every year, they come and go as though Papua New Guinea is their home.

The government gives them a visa for a six-pack of beer and citizenship for living here only three years. In my view, these Chinese businesses should be removed from the country for they sell low quality goods, pay low wages to locals, operate filthy shops and send money out of the country.

Let me expand upon each of these points in turn.

First, these Chinese shops sell low quality goods. Their prices are very tempting to the general public and it satisfies the demand of the people. However at the end, those goods last for a day or so and are a waste.

If you want to return them to the shop, the Chinese man will show you a big notice hanging on the side draped in cobwebs saying *'Choose Carefully! No Refund'*. They stick up notices like that for they know their goods do not last long since they were exported as waste from China.

Last week a friend of mine bought a nice looking phone for about K100 at a Chinese shop. It lasted for three days when the speaker stopped working properly. So he went to the shop to get a refund and told the shop assistant, a local girl, what was wrong with the phone.

Whilst they were talking, this Chinese man saw them and asked what was happening. The girl told him. The

Chinese man showed him the notice and sent him away threatening them to call the police.

Just one example of what has been happening to the general public.

Secondly, Chinese businesses in PNG and Bougainville pay low wages to their employees. In non-Chinese shops, shop assistants dress well whereas the Chinese employees dress as if they are going to work in the garden. They are only teenagers, mostly girls.

"We are not paid the normal rate others are paid," a shop assistant said. "We work because we have no place to get money."

She continued that if they complain about wages, the boss will tell them, 'I don't need you. I can get Chinese men to work.'

This is a serious issue that part of the country's workforce is facing. It is causing more Chinese to illegally migrate into PNG to work for such businesses.

Our government should do something about these young people for many of these Chinese store owners do not care about their employees. They should be removed from the region.

Thirdly, the shops are filthy and dusty. Throughout all the towns of Papua New Guinea where Chinese shops are, you will recognize them before you enter because even the walls outside are filthy and decaying.

Inside the shop, the goods are decorated with dust and cobwebs. It is like coming into a house which has been deserted for many years. Even new stock looks as if it is from last year. You always need to check the expiry date of food before buying.

But the public just buys stuff as it's not expensive.

My last big argument with Chinese businesses is the sending of the money back to China. Our country needs money to circulate so it boosts the economy.

These Chinese businessmen stand at the counter and wait for the money. When a money bag is full, the boss will take it away into his small room and then come back to the counter to wait for another.

But where does it go? A friend who worked at the Bank of the South Pacific in Madang told me, "You will hardly see any Chinese person depositing money in the bank".

Chinese businesses have been flourishing throughout Papua New Guinea serving the majority of the citizens of the country and are gradually moving towards Bougainville. They should be removed from Bougainville and even PNG.

Walking out rich from the Bougainville government
Leonard Fong Roka

All Bougainvilleans of sound mind know that in the 1990s 20,000 people perished on our island as the result of a civil war in the name of freedom.

Our relatives' lives were lost for our island to be free from the claws of Papua New Guinea and its exploitation and subjugation of our land and people.

When our young men took up arms and violence in 1988 against the PNG national government, Bougainville Copper Limited and the illegal Papua New Guinean squatter settlers, we the people stood up for them with our hearts.

The sacrifice is not much recognised by our present day leaders. Post-conflict Bougainville is a massive fireball of opportunists tearing apart the Bougainville our people died to save.

The Autonomous Bougainville Government (ABG) budget is fast going beyond K300 million whilst tax collected by the Bougainville's Internal Revenue Commission is trailing behind. In 2013 it's predicted to be around K12 million.

Despite our ambition for nationhood and despite this alarming financial gap, our people still run around desiring compensation for crisis-created losses.

The few businessmen we have are reluctant to pay tax, loudly calling for compensation for all they lost amidst the ten-year old conflict.

We all lost.

As ordinary Bougainvilleans around my area, the Tumpusiong Valley near Panguna, see it, our politicians ignore the fact they are public figures who should lead the

Bougainville people by example to really respect the issues we fought and died for on our island.

To most of us, painfully observing the shit in Bougainville politics, many of our politicians and bureaucrats do not live by the values and directives of the offices they hold.

Many public officials are an eyesore and nuisance to the community. They do not uphold the principles our people died for, instead leading Bougainville into the realm of corruption and personal prestige and power.

In these desperate times, leadership is challenging since the people are also powerful, perhaps more powerful than the government itself.

The people in the Tumpusiong Valley vote people who are weak into power; or we get old timers who had not walked with us through the path of the crisis.

They easily put on PNG shoes to play the game since they do not share the vision of those of us who suffered.

Many ABG parliamentarians are noted by the ordinary people as looters of the public offices they hold.

For reasons well known to lawyers, I won't name names.

Many Bougainvilleans dream to lead Bougainville; yet they lack the power to influence and educate. It is about time Bougainvilleans start practicing leadership on their own families.

When Deputy Administrator Andrew Pisi died in 2007, his extended family members of Moroni village in Panguna came and ransacked the Administration office in Arawa.

They walked away with office materials like computers, furniture and a vehicle - nearly a million kina's worth of loot.

With the death of Chief Administrator, Peter Tsiamalili, in late 2007, his family appropriated his official vehicle; all efforts to get it returned failed.

This problem was also present with two former ABG presidents. Presidents have entitlements when leaving office but it should be noted that family members of the pair went beyond the entitlements.

When the first ABG president, Joseph Kabui, passed away in mid-2008, his official vehicle was locked at his residence in Hutjena as a bargaining tool for the release of entitlements. But when the entitlement was honoured, the ABG vehicle was not returned.

The question is: 'Are leaders and ordinary people interested in saving Bougainville for the benefit and betterment of future generations?'

Ordinary people of Bougainville struggle to make ends meet, yet our lazy leaders leave office with wealth and tell people their island needs more money to run.

With this trend, more money for the island will mean more corruption and possible derailing of Bougainville's progress to independence.

Can the current Bougainville President, John Momis, and Administrator, Raymond Masono, change this?

I wonder when the ABG will start getting out amongst the people of Bougainville and finding out what their thoughts are about their island.

Will the death penalty stop violent crime in PNG?
Albert Tobby

Violent crimes flourish unabated in our societies today. This is not recent practice but a continuation of violence of a similar nature over a prolonged period.

People don't just wake-up one morning and decide to rape or murder someone. They've developed a perspective over a period of time that shaped their world view and regulates their behaviour.

People's attitudes are shaped by their socio-cultural environment, their education and their genetic heredity.

However there are other mechanisms that ensure that these three elements function in shaping individual behaviour, such as economic and social services.

The absence of these supporting mechanisms will directly or indirectly weaken the role of the three elements (there is much literature on this in behavioural science).

Bishop Young correctly posits programs that support young men's meaningful engagement in the economy, including job creation and improving policing capacity to prevent crime.

We know that youth unemployment is high in Papua New Guinea (ADB 2012 and UNDP 2012). Drug abuse is rampant among unemployed youth including secondary school students.

Last year there were about 17,000 Grade 12 students graduating; only 4,000 gained admission to the tertiary institutions. Where are the majority, the 13,000 graduates, now?

Transport infrastructure has deteriorated from bad to worse in many rural areas (and in some urban centres) limiting access to markets and better health services.

The ratio of certified medical doctors to patients in PNG is 1:10,000 (Global Health Foundation 2010) and nurses to patients 0.5:1,000 (OECD, 2012).

In 2004 the Police Commission reported there are only 5,250 regular police officers, a police to population ration of 1:1,121.

The structure, size and deployment of regular police have remained unchanged since independence - completely oblivious to the growing population. These statistics and many more point to the reasons why our law and order problems are perpetuated with such ferocity.

I doubt the death penalty will deter violent crime in this country if these underlying issues are not addressed effectively by the respective responsible authorities and institutions.

Grass-fruits! Inspiring stories of community self-help
Emma Wakpi

13/11/12 -14:14:37hrs - Emma I landed in pop now...
21:29:26hrs – Left pop 4pm and arrived 9pm now - drived on a
roughy road n arrived now at Afore - overnight and get home
tomorrow
14/11/12 - 14:40:08hrs – Leaving Afore on a hire car going to
Itokama... 16:48:52hrs – ARIVED NOW ITOKAMA

So wrote John Kumbo, a bible translator of the Barai tribe (population 5,000) and chairman of the Barai Non Formal Education Association (BNEA).

He had been in Goroka attending a consultation network comprising various government and non-government organisations whose common bond is "holistic transformation" using CHE (Community Health Evangelism developed by Medical Ambassadors International) as the tool to facilitate community development.

And it was not only John who had travelled great distances. The United Church Health Services of Milne Bay had three representatives who braved rough seas to travel from Salamo, Ferguson Island.

Manus Provincial Health Department also sent representatives as did the newly formed Jiwaka Province.

Other people came from the settlements of Port Moresby, the mountains of Chimbu and Eastern Highlands.

Joseph Sukwianomb from the Prime Ministers Department (Director 20/50 Vision sector) chose the rather humble meeting over the National Health Conference that was being held in the same week.

The theme of the fifth annual conference held in Kefamo EHP from 4-7 November was "be prepared for the unexpected, be prepared for surprises" and the accompanying Bible text was taken from Joshua.

It was felt that too often we focus to on the accomplishment of our goals without taking into account the unexpected ripple effects that impact individuals and communities in various ways.

At the conclusion of the meeting, I came away in awe at the amazing work carried out by unlikely heroes in various areas of Papua New Guinea.

These people see development as their responsibility and have raised their hands to do something about it.

There really were surprising and unexpected stories told and, as we approach Christmas and remember that this season is about love and the pouring out of oneself for the betterment of mankind, these individuals epitomized that.

For them their work is more than a job or something to gain; for them it is about the love of their fellow man and the sharing of their knowledge and abilities so that "peace and goodwill to men" can be realised.

Here are some of my summaries of what for me were highlights of this year's conference.

Barai Non Formal Education Association: 21 villages working for their own prosperity [John Kumbo]

Mr Kumbo told of how 10 years of constant community interaction using CHE materials (which he and his team translated into their language) had seen marked improvements in combating malnutrition, increased immunisation (almost 100%) and almost 100% literacy. The whole language group of 21 villages in Afore district of Oro Province has been affected.

In addition to the CHE translated booklets, John and his team have also translated booklets teaching on cooking, agriculture and budgeting. As a result of this there has been reconciliation among groups of people with the 21 villages.

A ripple effect of this endeavour has been that they have now registered an association, Afore Hope for the Disabled and are teaching from the CHE lessons on disability looking at how they can better integrate the disabled into their communities, allowing them to actively participate in community life and decision making processes.

Living Light Four Square in Port Moresby: Fearless mother combating TB in Moresby settlements [Egma Mua]

Egma is a mother of five children (aged 2 to 16) and is a volunteer from Four Square Living Light Church in Kaugere who has been working in settlements near the church, where CHE volunteers (settlement residents) are also trained in TB DOTS (Direct Observation of Treatment Shortcourse).

The CHE volunteers each find a TB patient in their own settlement, take them to the health centre, and each day observe their taking the TB medicine for six months. For this they receive a small monthly allowance of K70.

With this amazing program of 300 volunteers some communities are now clean of tuberculosis. Egma now gives a five-minute time slot each Sunday between worship and the sermon for a health talk which so far focuses on the major issue of TB.

Egma has been doing this work for nearly six years using her own time and resources. She travels around on PMVs and walks the notorious settlements of Port Moresby with her volunteers.

She related a story of when she was at Koki market and about to get on a PMV when she was dragged back by a youth. The young man gently held onto her and told her to wait.

As she waited, watching a couple of youths go around picking pockets, she asked the young man if they had ever met. He replied, "*Yu no save long mi tasol mama mi save long yu na wok yu mekim*" ('You don't know me, mama, but I know the work you do').

He then helped her into the bus and went on his way.

Kundiawa Pastors' Orphan Care initiative (Orkids) [Pastor Felix]

After our conference in 2011, Egma went to her village of Om Kolai in the Gumine district of Simbu Province. She felt that, while she was doing good things in Port Moresby, her own community could also benefit from this training. She met with pastors and leaders from 18 churches and conducted a three-day workshop.

In looking at issues in their community, praying and doing house-to-house surveys, the pastors realised that adopted children (orphans or single parent children) were neglected by the families caring for them, resulting in 200 malnourished and unschooled kids.

Girls barely reaching puberty were pregnant and drug and alcohol abuse was high. Pastor Felix, as chairman, drew up a schedule to share the load for a three times a week program of Bible teaching, feeding a healthy meal, teaching carers about hygiene and cleanliness, distributing used clothing, and taking turns to make sure the kids went to school. Some have been taken in by the pastors' families.

In discussing whether a care centre might be a good idea, the group urged them not to warehouse kids, but to work with their families to help improve living conditions and to teach about cultivating crops so they don't lose the land they have a right to own.

St Mary's Catholic Parish, Goroka – A vibrant congregation impacting their neighbours [Joyce Kuias]

Joyce Kuias is a full time mum taking care of her paraplegic son and two primary school children, yet she still finds time to teach kindergarten classes, nutritional cooking lessons for mothers and to help train cell groups in CHE healthy home lessons.

Joyce, together with her priest Fr John Ryan, have so far established 146 healthy homes in the settlements. They have also encouraged their church members to know their HIV status. Joyce and her husband along with Fr Ryan were the first to get tested.

They are continuing to encourage young couples who want to marry to know their HIV status and to continue counselling once their status is known.

The CHE program has influenced the whole church around Goroka and has extended to more congregations as their small groups study the Bible together and encourage Bible reading in every home, reach out to the poor and establish healthy homes. Joyce is now also teaching sports teams and children's groups in holistic development.

Amazing Grace: Wilberforce & Papua New Guinea
Emma Wakpi

Watching the movie *Amazing Grace* about the life and work of William Wilberforce made me curious to learn more. So I turned to Wikipedia and was struck by a brief summary of his life philosophy - *"Wilberforce was convinced of the importance of religion, morality and education."*

Wilberforce of course was instrumental in the abolition of the slave trade in Great Britain. What a life: to be convinced of an ideal and to pursue it despite the backlash and threat of being ostracised from society.

But there were other things about my own country that I gleaned from this movie.

Wilberforce was a good man but he required challenge and support to do the right thing. He was an impressionable young man with good intentions. He had a moral conscience and wanted to do the right thing.

He was pushed to use his position and influence for the greater good of society by the influence of an old school teacher, John Newton, and also, when Wilberforce became a parliamentarian, by various associates who believed strongly in causes such as abolition of the slave trade, education and the humane treatment of animals.

John Newton himself is known as the writer of arguably the most famous hymn on earth, *Amazing Grace*. He had captained a ship involved in the slave trade and later in life was converted.

He influenced Wilberforce in his formative college years, to make him aware of the moral wrongs committed by society. Although Wilberforce was aware and felt bad about the slave trade, he did not believe he could do anything about it.

However he was challenged and became convinced to do something; others were willing to stand with him and support him to do the right thing.

Reflecting on the situation in Papua New Guinea, there is a lot of talk and assessing of leaders in various government bodies from the National Parliament right down to the local level government.

But, when it comes time to do the work, a lot of sage advice is given from the sidelines to the leaders without commitment of time, finance or other resources to help them. When they fail, criticism is heaped upon them and knowing nods and looks exchanged about how we just *knew* they couldn't make it.

As I am writing this, good young leaders like Garry Juffa come to mind as well as our three women leaders, Loujaya Tony, Delilah Gore and Julie Soso. We recognise in them the willingness and drive to get the work done and to do it right.

The onus is now upon us as groups and individuals within the electorate (and the greater society) in which they are operating to lend our support and services in order for them to create policies and protocols that can be respected and followed.

If we are serious about gender equity gaining momentum, we will help support our women leaders in any way we can so that they are successful in what they do.

If we are serious about transparency and accountability we will come out in support of issues raised in parliament by Garry Juffa and write to him and let him know he is not alone.

We need to garner support around them etc. Individuals who can do something must go ahead and do it and support our leaders so that they can go on to do greater things for our electorates, province and country.

All this cannot happen if we as individuals and agencies are not convinced about the issues they are raising. We must be convinced of an issue and then pursue the achievement of this issue. We cannot expect our leaders to find us but must make ourselves available to them.

Should they refuse our help we continue what we are doing and hope to find another who can take up our cause if they choose to work with us we must be committed and give our all so that goals and ideals are realised.

In his pursuit of what he believed was right, Wilberforce was willing to face the contempt of his contemporaries and society. What impresses and challenges me about Wilberforce is the fact he took up the cause at the risk of being ostracised by his own people and best friends - even risking his life. He was young, just 21, he was wealthy, he was in the higher echelon of society; he could have just enjoyed his life yet, when he was convinced, he pursued his convictions.

Sometimes Papua New Guineans worst enemies are those within. Those that are educated and can make a difference and have the means but just don't care or are so encumbered by the expectations of their culture that it disarms or even stomps out every good intention.

Almost everyone you meet will state emphatically that they have religion, morality and education and value its importance; however very few will be convinced to the point of risking their lives or risk being ostracised by family and clan to pursue their ideals.

So there is a lot of talk, but very few people in PNG can make a moral decision and stick with it when it is pitted against the goliath of custom and culture.

The time is coming when individuals will have to take a stand. The burning of a young mother last month highlights the reality of what can be at stake should one choose to do the right thing. Pursuing one's conviction can call for a high level of moral and physical courage.

In a society where fear and lack of education create powerful emotional responses, one has to be convinced of an issue in order to stand up against the status quo.

Governments can enact laws but this does not necessarily equate with respect and adherence in those whom it's meant to regulate.

To attain lasting change, individuals must be persuaded to challenge the cultural norms which prevent the growth of a healthy society.

This must be done in the realisation that decisions made will not only reflect upon the individual but the family, clan and tribe. The cost must be spelt out and each person made aware of the consequence of the decisions.

If like-minded people can get together from each clan it would be a start in addressing some of our current social issues.

Better education will tackle social issues in PNG
Joe Wasia

Do we have any coherent plans and strategies to combat tribal fights and other violent social unrest which are too common in Papua New Guinea?

I believe education would be a greatest tool to solve these issues in our country - and most of our people are really lacking an education.

The vast majority of Papua New Guineans, more than 70%, still live in rural areas where there is no proper education. As a result, we have an uneducated population with many social issues.

Tribal fights, as mentioned by Francis Nii in a recent article and similar social issues we discuss and read about at *PNG Attitude* and other media, are very common in much of PNG society where there is no proper education, health and other basic infrastructure.

Successive governments have neglected this vast majority, their focus diverted to the main centres of the country. And that was really unfair for the people.

Rural societies need support from the responsible authorities. The national, provincial and local level governments, NGOs, business houses, international agencies and organisations must support students and educated youths to conduct awareness in rural villages on pressing issues such as warfare, elections, HIV/AIDS, education, global warming, etc.

This will bring some change to community, provinces and country. The students and youths will be engaged so they can be advocates for social peace and order. As we know, young people have the potential to do harm or good and that is where a change for the better needs to start.

Government must invest more in human resource development. Establish schools, subsidise schooling, get more school age kids enrolled and provide more employment opportunities for the growing population.

I know education can play a greater role in maintaining peace and order in the societies throughout the country. Being educated doesn't mean a bachelor's degree; it means you do things well and think better than others. And that's where change starts.

As a member of the educated elite in my society, I know I would not tolerate tribal fights or other social disorder in my society nor support perpetrators in any way.

I know that education has shaped the way I think and act. Education has changed me to be who I'm and given me a bright future. That's how it helps keep societies in order when change starts from an individual through education.

We can deploy armed security, police and even defence force to tribal areas to contain fights and social unrest but they will never solve the problem. Trouble will still erupt because people are uneducated.

As the great Nelson Mandela said: "Education is the most powerful weapon which you can use to change the world." Yes, we can change Papua New Guinea through education.

On police brutality & police theft in Papua New Guinea
Ganjiki D Wayne

Multiple reports surface every week of some rogue police activity in our country.

Drivers gets 'accidentally' shot in the foot. Arbitrary confiscation (and then consumption) of informal vendors' property. Theft of wallets and personal property. 'Fines' for concocted traffic offences (such as driving too slowly in a car park).

Private armed escort for politicians, foreign businessmen and corrupt bureaucrats. And of course the regular brutal beatings (and sometimes slaying) of innocent citizens and surrendered crime suspects.

It seems endless what abuses our "law-enforcers-slash-disciplined-force" can cook up. More than half of all of the Solicitor General's defence of claims against the State are police brutality claims.

These are men and women who seem to have lost all moral restraint. There's a vacuum in their mindset and conscience. They lack the ability to put themselves in the shoes of their prey.

They have no concern for their own and their victims' dignity. Nor for the respectability and the integrity of the office and uniform they occupy. Nor loyalty to their Commissioner (who recently spoke strongly against such rogue behaviour), the Constabulary, or the Nation.

They have no fear of God. No regard for their code of ethics. How they sleep at night I don't know. I suspect they drink themselves to sleep; to shut out the voices of conviction that keep ringing in their heads.

They got into the uniform for all the wrong reasons (it's just bread and butter). These are toddlers in adult bodies.

Worse, the State (we the people) clothed these toddlers with the vicarious authority to pull-up any vehicle or person simply by waving their colours and displaying their arms. And we the people agreed to subject ourselves to their authority. We got more than we bargained for.

Toddlers. Babies. Whose world revolves around "me", they cry for milk you must give. They hunger, you feed. They thirst, you give water. They hurt, you comfort. They freeze, you warm. They soil their diapers, you must clean them up. They cry, you soothe. They take, you give.

That is the nature of infants. Despite adult bodies we lack the emotional intelligence to subject ourselves to codes that should provide restraint. We are a nation of toddlers. And a lot of them wear blue and carry not-toy guns. (A hundred or so sit in parliament accusing each other of wetting their diapers.)

The problem isn't the training (or lack of) that they get, or a lack of understanding of the law and human rights. That's a scratch above the surface. The real lack is the loss of moral consciousness.

And so the real challenge is to refill those gaps. The crimes committed are completely identifiable as crimes (theft, assault, unlawful use of firearm, murder), and as blatant evil deeds.

Any sane person should be able to tell that the unlawful use of his authority to steal wallets and personal effects is an immoral deed; an attack on basic human decency; even an undermining of his own human dignity as the perpetrator. But it takes a person of moral strength to resist committing those crimes.

These are men and women who have lost that moral strength. And many involved in talking about social correction wouldn't want the work that's needed to restore such a loss. We'd rather not go that deep.

We'd rather a social correction (a fleeting band-aid solution). Or a legal one (guess who will enforce!). Or an academic one (with never-ending papers and opinions). Or a training one (where we try to squeeze a lifetime of lessons into six months!). Or a governmental one (where we assume the Minister can flick his fingers for a solution).

We agree that wrong is wrong. It's mostly our solutions to those wrongs that take diverging paths.

Maybe they're frustrated with the meagre pay they get. Perhaps coupled with the pressures of life they're driven to such measures for survival. It's understandable. Is it? Lack of training perhaps? Lack of knowledge of human rights?

Ever noticed how our behaviour is little affected by what we know? Ignorance of the law?

Whatever reason we give, we'll have to settle that ultimately it's the loss of moral strength in these people's souls that gives them no pause against such crimes.

And if there is to be any proper solution, it must begin at the core of their moral beliefs. We need to restore that moral strength. Everything else will be band-aid.

I know good cops. But for every good cop I know there's probably 50 not-so-good cops.

We live in a nation where the sight of an armed policeman or a police land-cruiser with tinted-windows strikes more fear in an ordinary citizen than a lonely drive into a crime-prone suburb.

Recall that crawl up your spine as you approach a tinted cop-car? The source of terror is reversed. No longer is it the local terrorist. It's the law enforcers who are supposed to catch that terrorist.

Drivers don't trust police road checks anymore. Victims of crime dismiss the thought of contacting police as they contemplate how vain such an effort would be. Reports to the internal complaints unit might as well be lottery tickets for a zillion kina.

No. A restoration of proper morals is needed. But there are problems with a moral-restoration approach. It's hard work.

And post-modern philosophy would disagree. Post-modern philosophies that subscribe to an amoral universe would say that we should just fix society and these people will adjust with society. But to fix society you have to fix these people. A catch-22.

We would have to take the discussion all the way back to the nature of morality and who would give such guidance. And there lies our problem.

I could suggest get the Church to counsel these cops. But then the debate will turn to the delusional question of separation of church and State.

And of course people would argue that the Church has obviously failed because these cops probably attend church every week and have gotten nowhere. So let's leave it at bandaid level.

So you would suggest get the shrinks and mental disorder experts to counsel them. Bring in the social scientists.

Impose the name tags. Name and shame. Step up police discipline. Extend training. Informing human rights. Up their pay. Dock their pay. Demote. Transfer. Recruit smarter people. Remove silly people. Take away the guns. Give them Tramontinas. Take away the vehicles. Give them Landcruisers. Install CCTV everywhere. Bring the Aussies. Bring the Fijians. Send our people to Aussieland. Send them to Fiji. Send them to Iraq. Send them to college. Send them home. Don't send them at all.

Band-aids.

The best solution is usually the hardest.

Beyond 'bisnis blo mi': Redefining the public service
Bernard Yegiora

There is a growing culture that I really dislike in the Papua New Guinea public service. Most public servants treat the public organisation as their private business.

When some are in a position of authority, they try their best to remove people who are a threat to their position. Smart people with bright ideas are the ones who get fired, or worse, put on a leash.

Unlike a small privately-run business where you can remain the manager for life, public servants do not have that luxury.

Thus, what is the rationale behind eliminating your threat when you are replaceable as well?

Sometimes bureaucratic politics do not make sense when you are an outsider trying to analyse what is happening.

For departments that deal with money, funds for projects are either diverted into their personal accounts or they ask for a 10% commission for being the middle man who helped facilitate the release of the funds.

Is that the right thing to do?

Lateness is another issue that is at the heart of this growing culture. Some public servants think that they can bounce into the office at any time of the day and go out for lengthy lunch breaks.

There is now a new trend where public servants who are suspended because of serious allegations are using the courts to get stay orders so they can remain in office while investigations are carried out.

If you are still in office, it means you can use the resources at your disposal to hamper investigative efforts.

The normal process is to step aside and let the investigators in the form of auditors do their auditing. Their reports will determine whether or not you, as the accused, have a case to answer.

One particular public servant in one of the provinces when suspended from office told everyone that "*em birthright blo mi, mi mamapapa ground*" (it is my birth right because this is my land).

What is the meaning of this statement?

The public service is not a private, regional, provincial, or tribal business. It was established to serve the seven million citizens of this young nation.

No wonder it is very difficult nowadays to appoint someone from one of the island provinces to work up in the highlands as the provincial administrator or serve in other positions of authority.

In addition, from my observation concepts like professionalism and meritocracy are slowly giving way to cronyism and wantokism.

During the orientation week this year at Divine Word University, I was amazed when my head of department for the PNG Studies Department told the first year students that, "This is my office for now, but in a few years this might be your office, so feel free to come in".

You will rarely hear a statement of that nature in the public service.

Each and every public servant need to change their mind set, if we want to see changes in line with the Vision 2050.

The Writers

Some of Our Authors

Kela Kapkora Sil Bolkin was born in the Galkope area in the Simbu Province. He studied to become a Catholic priest but quit soon after completing his philosophical studies and attended the UPNG where he completed a BA majoring in Social Development and Anthropology. He also has a certificate of Leadership in Strategic Health Communication from the Johns Hopkins University (USA). He is now the Senior Policy Analyst at the National AIDS Council Secretariat in Port Moresby. His work appeared in the 2011 Crocodile Prize anthology and he currently has a book about Simbu men's houses with the publisher Crawford House.

Michael Dom was born in Port Moresby. He graduated from the University of Papua New Guinea and now works as an agricultural scientist for a government organisation. He says he writes poetry because he likes to have his say. He also feels that poetry is often underestimated as a powerful means of expression for the collective conscience of people. His work was published in the 2011 and 2012 Crocodile Competition Anthologies. In 2012 he won the Crocodile Prize for poetry.

Jeffrey Mane Febi comes from Simbu Province. He is a geologist working in the oil and gas industry and lives with his wife and child in Port Moresby. Writing and reading are his favourite hobbies and he has had some success in publishing his work locally. He is an accomplished poet and writer and won the 2011 Crocodile Prize for a short story.

Megghan Zeriga Jimbudo is currently in Grade 11 at Paradise High School in Port Moresby. He is from mixed Oro and Morobe parentage and likes reading and listening to music. He spent the early part of his life in Wewak and completed Grade 10 at Bumayong Lutheran Secondary School in Lae.

Gary Juffa is the Governor of Northern Province. He was formerly PNG's Customs Commissioner, a role he occupied for five years following 10 years as a customs officer. He is widely credited with transforming the department into a highly efficient organisation. He is a thinker and a writer with a clear idea of his mission. He wrote earlier this year: "Leaders are elected to serve, promote and protect the interests of their people, those who elected them into parliament for that purpose."

David Kitchnoge was born in Kainantu in the Eastern Highlands Province. His parents come from the East Sepik and Morobe Provinces. He is a graduate of the Divine Word University in Madang and is a financial manager living in Port Moresby. He regards himself as a rural product and is very passionate about rural development issues.

Mary Avia Koisen lives in Port Moresby and works for Telikom PNG as an account executive for mining, petroleum and gas companies. She enjoys writing whenever she reaches an emotional high. She also loves art and expressions of feelings through paintings and hopes to one day take up art and learn to paint.

Erick Kowa was born in Kaut on New Ireland. His father came from West Sepik and worked for Burns Philp. In 1991, after a stint on Bougainville, his family went to live at Wara Kongkong, outside Vanimo. He went to Green River High School and then St Ignatius Secondary School in Aitape. He studied Chemical Engineering on a scholarship at the University of Queensland and worked for Oilsearch as a Petroleum Engineer until 2009. He completed a Master's Degree in Oil and Gas Engineering at the University of Aberdeen in Scotland while on a British Chevening Scholarship. After that he was employed by IPA, an American consulting house, successively in London, Washington and

Singapore, as a Capital Project Analyst for Upstream Oil and Gas Exploration and Production.

Lapieh Landu was born in Port Moresby of mixed Eastern Highlands, Milne Bay and Sanduan parentage. She has completed an Arts degree at the Divine Word University in Madang studying international relations. She is someone who realises the need for culture and traditions to be captured and maintained through writing but also its importance in today's technological society. She was the inaugural winner of the 2011 Crocodile Prize for Women's Literature.

Martyn Awayang Namorong was born at Baimuru in the Gulf Province and grew up in a logging camp at Kamusi on the border between Western and Gulf Provinces. His parents come from Madang and Western Province. He was a medical student at UPNG until 2009 but is now 'Papua New Guinea's most controversial blogger'. He won the 2011 Crocodile Prize for an essay. He works as a journalist and presenter for EMTV.

Francis Sina Nii was born at Yobai, Karimui Nomane in the Simbu Province. He has a degree in economics from UPNG and was a banker with the National Development Bank until an accident left him paraplegic. He is now a patient of the Kundiawa General Hospital. He has had an interest in writing since his UPNG days. He was an entrant in both the 2011 and 2012 Crocodile Prize Competition and his work features in the anthologies for those years. He recently published a novel called *Fitman, Raitman and Cooks: Paradise in Peril.*

Ishmael Palipal is from Koromira in the Kokoda District of Central Bougainville. He was born during the peak of Bougainville Crisis in the small village of Koianu, south of Koromira, in 1992. He is in his second year studying Social and Religious Studies at Divine Word University. He likes writing, reading, telling stories, listening to people, taking photos and making music.

Leonard Fong Roka was born in Arawa and grew up in the Panguna District during the years of the Bougainville crisis. He began writing poetry as a student at Arawa High School and has now compiled a collection of short stories and poetry which he hopes to publish. He has returned after a break as a student at Divine Word University and is working on an autobiography of his experiences in the Bougainville war in his spare time. He had some of his earlier work published in both the 2011 and 2012 Crocodile Competition Anthologies. He has recently published a book of poetry called *The Pomong U'tau of Dreams* and will soon publish a book of short stories.

Pamela Josephine Toliman is the Laboratory Research Coordinator for the HIV and STI Laboratory within the Sexual and Reproductive Health Unit of the Papua New Guinea Institute of Medical Research. She has worked in this field for nearly ten years. She is the mother of two wonderful children.

Emma Tunne Wakpi is from Tombil in the Minj District of Jiwaka Province. She is a business graduate and community development worker with Evangelical Brotherhood Church Health Establishment based in Goroka. Emma says she was discouraged from pursuing a career in writing by her family due to the "lack of opportunities" it afforded. "However, I have always been interested in writing," she says, "especially essays and poetry and in my spare time try to write and have done so since 2006." She won the Crocodile Prize for Women's Literature in 2012.

Joe Wasia is from the Wapenamanda district of the Enga Province. He studied Environmental Health Sciences at Divine Word University in Madang, majoring in Occupational Health & Safety, He began writing for *PNG Attitude* about four years ago. He is interested in politics, business, reading novels, music (R&B, pop, hip hop) and telling stories.

Martinez Wasuak is a Year 4 student in the Department Of PNG Studies and International Relations at Divine Word University in Madang.

Bernard Yegiora was born in Kundiawa but his heritage is in Kubalia, East Sepik Province. His grandfather was one of the early colonial policemen from the coast who helped the Administration build the highway to the highlands. Here he found his wife to be in the Sinasina village of Koge, Simbu Province. Bernard started writing for the *Sunday Chronicle* in Mathew Yakai's *Letters from China* column in 2009 when he left for China to study. He hopes to one day publish a book about politics in PNG. After obtaining his MA he began teaching politics and international relations at Divine Word University in Madang.

Cover Designer

Joe Bilbu is a surf wear designer in Fiji who originally comes from Babaka village in Central Province. He completed his primary education at St Peters School in Erima and his secondary school at De la Salle High, Bomana, before moving to Arawa High in Bougainville, and finally Passam National High School in the East Sepik. He has a Diploma of Graphic Design from the National Arts School and a Certificate in Electronic Publishing from RMIT in Melbourne. He is married to a Fijian citizen and has three children.

www.ingramcontent.com/pod-product-compliance
Lightning Source LLC
Chambersburg PA
CBHW070921130626

46555CB00001B/230